Who were the Pharaohs?

WHO WERE THE
PHARAOHS?

A history of their names with a list of cartouches

Stephen Quirke

with cartouches drawn by Richard Parkinson

Dover Publications, Inc.
Mineola, New York

Acknowledgements

I am greatly indebted to all members of the Department of Egyptian Antiquities at the British Museum for their help and advice, and most particularly to Dr Richard Parkinson for drawing the cartouches for Chapter 5. I thank also the Metropolitan Museum of Art, New York, and the Museo Gregoriano in the Vatican Museums for permission to reproduce the photographs on pp. 28 and 38 respectively.

Third impression 1996

Originally published by British Museum Publications Ltd
46 Bloomsbury Street, London WC1B 3QQ

Library of Congress Cataloging-in-Publication Data
Quirke, Stephen
    Who were the pharoahs? : a history of their names
with a list of cartouches/Stephen Quirke; with
cartouches drawn by Richard Parkinson.
      p.   cm.
    Includes bibliographical references and index.
    ISBN 0–486–26586–2 (pbk.)
    1. Pharaohs   2. Names, Personal—Egyptian.
    I. Title.
DT61.Q57   1990
932′.00992—dc20   90-13808
                                          CIP

Designed by Andrew Shoolbred

Printed and bound in Great Britain

Cover Gold openwork plaque of
Amenemhat IV, shown offering unguent to the
creator Atum. Perhaps from Byblos.
Height 2.8 cm. EA 59194.

Page 2 Lower part of a statue, showing the
cartouches of Ramses II granted life by the sun-
god. Height 98 cm. EA 27.

Contents

Acknowledgements
4

Introduction
6

1 The five names of Pharaoh
9

2 The emergence of the fivefold titulary, *c.*3000–2000 BC
20

3 The classic titulary, *c.*2000–1000 BC
29

4 Variations: the elaborate and the pure, *c.*1300–30 BC
34

5 The principal names of the kings of Egypt
44

Biblography
79

Index
80

Introduction

Naming kings of Egypt in English

Egyptologists group the kings of Egypt according to the scheme of a history written in the third century BC by an Egyptian priest called Manetho. Only summaries and extracts of Manetho's works survive, but we know from these that he divided the kings who ruled Egypt before the arrival of Alexander the Great in 332 BC into 'dynasties'. Each dynasty comprised kings who shared a common town, either as the place of origin or burial, or as capital city. Kings belonging to the same family might also be grouped separately, but family ties seem secondary in the scheme of Manetho. In general, the plan of about thirty dynasties corresponds to groupings of kings from the ancient sources, and for that reason the terms 'Dynasty 1' to 'Dynasty 30' or '31' are still used. Sometimes a dynasty in Manetho's history cannot be identified as a separate group in ancient Egyptian records. In such cases the 'dynasty' may result not from a separate group of kings but from a reinterpretation by an ancient historian or from a mistake by a scribe copying out an older kinglist. To cover uncertainties Egyptologists use broader terms in addition to the narrower dynasties, and denote periods of unity as 'kingdoms', and periods of disunity as 'intermediate periods'. In the Old, Middle and New Kingdoms, and again in the Late Period, Egypt was united under an Egyptian king ruling over all the land between the First Cataract and the Delta of the river Nile. In between those years of unity Egypt was divided among rival kinglets or occupied by foreign powers.

The ancient Egyptian scripts recorded only the consonantal skeleton of words. As in modern Hebrew and Arabic, vowels were expendable and could be supplied by the informed speaker. Today the people of Egypt speak Arabic, and their ancient language is dead, with the result that vowels in ancient Egyptian can be supplied only through indirect means. Of these the most direct is Coptic, where the Greek script, including vowels, is adapted for the Egyptian language, mainly for Christian texts. Another store of vowels for Egyptian words comes from cuneiform, the script used for a series of languages in the ancient Near East. The cuneiform script includes vowels, and cuneiform texts sometimes provide writings of Egyptian words, generally names. Greek writings also offer a variety of forms for Egyptian words, again mainly names, with vowels. Unfortunately all scripts reproduce sound according to local convention, and the vowels in Egyptian words among Coptic, cuneiform and Greek texts may be distorted either by the conventions of the particular script or by differences in pronunciation. As a result there is little consistency in attempts to put Egyptian names into our modern scripts. Some authors use name forms adapted from Coptic or selected from Greek variants, while others take the ancient Egyptian skeleton word and add a token glide-vowel where necessary. This booklet opts for the latter, in the hope of remaining close to the ancient writings if not the ancient speech. The examples below illustrate the range of possibilities. The sound values in the table are taken directly from hieroglyphic writings of the names, and letters between brackets denote sounds not always included in those writings.

Sound value	English from Greek	English from Egyptian
ḥw.f-w(i)	Cheops	Khufu
ḥ'.f-r'	Chephren	Khafra
mn-k3w-r'	Mycerinus	Menkaura
ppy	Phiops	Pepy
ḫty	Achthoes	Khety
imn-m-ḥ3t	Ammenemes	Amenemhat
s-n-wsrt	Sesostris	Senusret
dḥwty-ms	Tuthmosis	Thutmose
3ḫ-n-itn	no form used	Akhenaten
ḥr-m-ḥb	Harmais	Horemheb
st(ḫ)y	Sethos	Sety
r'-ms-sw	Ramesses	Ramses
p3-sb3-ḫ'-n-niwt	Psusennes	Pasebakhaenniut
psmṭk	Psammetichus	Psamtek

1

The five names of Pharaoh

Naming represents a first step in language, a first sign that man stands apart from the world around. Giving things names permits us to order our world by distinguishing each item in our experience: without names the material world would become an uncontrolled sea of matter. In some religions the absence of names represents a condition of bliss or heaven, but for every known society that condition provides no workable alternative to living with names. People are no exception to the law of naming. Both society and the individual need some means of expressing the identity of a person distinct from all other members of the group, for without a label of identity a person cannot be singled out for praise or censure, and order would be lost. Every human society confers identity on each of its members at birth, in the form of personal names. Our names express the individual in each of us, on the terms of the society in which we live. In ancient Egypt name giving usually involved one name, given at birth by the parents of the child. Later in life many Egyptians acquired a second name, not as regularly as the modern English surname, but more occasionally in the manner of our nicknames and middle names.

In Egypt the name of a thing or person did more than express identity, it *incorporated* identity. Whoever knew the names of things or people knew their entire being. Therefore the ancient Egyptian equivalent of an encyclopaedia would begin with a claim to provide knowledge of everything that exists, but it would consist simply of a list of names of objects and places, without any definitions or explanations: the name would carry within itself the knowledge. Names could also confer power over the thing or person named. At the gates of the underworld the deceased needed to know the names of the guardian demons and all their armoury of magic in order to pass through to eternal life. The name was part of the essence of a person, explicit in personal names such as Renseneb ('May my name be well') and Renefankh ('May his [the child's] name live'). The idea survives into the latest period of ancient Egyptian culture with the religious formula titled 'May my name flourish'. Donors of tombstones and statues called themselves 'those who made the name (of the beneficiary) live', meaning live forever, and one of the spells for the dead in the New Kingdom, the so-called 'Book of the Dead', bears the title 'Spell for causing the name of the deceased to be remembered in the afterlife'. Conversely, the loss of the personal name implied annihilation. Traitors were branded 'woe to his name' and forfeited their birth names. The palace conspirators who were found guilty of poisoning Ramses III in *c.*1150 BC had their names distorted into curses, for

Stela of an official named Sedpepy ('kingship festival of Pepy'). Height 58 cm. EA 1818.

example, from Ramessu ('Ra is his creator') into Ramesdedsu ('Ra is his hater'). Disgrace for a man might bring the removal of his name from all monuments, to deprive him of the magical afterlife secured by the hieroglyphs. Equally, a man might take over another's statue simply by replacing the names on it with his own, a favourite practice of kings conscious of the cost of new monuments. By contrast, faces on statues are less often remodelled; a name established identity more securely than the generalised image.

At birth a future king of Egypt would receive a personal name in the same way that every Egyptian acquired his or her label of identity. For the king of Egypt a second name became necessary when he came to power, in order to express his new identity as king. For two and a half thousand years, from the Pyramid Age to the last of the Ptolemies, kings of Egypt received five names, four at accession and one at birth. These names followed a traditional order from the Middle Kingdom onwards, and each name was introduced by a special royal title. The titles of the royal names were, in the classic order:

> Horus
> He of the Two Ladies
> (Horus of) Gold
> He of the Sedge and Bee
> Son of Ra

The last title, son of Ra, introduced the birth name of the king. All five titles and the first four names were taken at the installation of the king, to distinguish him from ordinary human beings. The clothing, diadems, sceptres and thrones performed the same function of setting the king of Egypt apart from mankind and closer to the gods. Yet the titled names did not merely denote sovereignty: they included the essence of kingship and, in the names themselves, the identity of that king.

Although kingship beliefs evolved across the three thousand years of their existence, at all periods two ideas dominate the royal names. In the first place ancient Egypt was not a single but a double land, and her rulers by extension bore a twofold nature. Secondly, the king stood between gods and men, with the power of gods but the mortality of mankind.

A single state with one ruler appeared c.3000 BC Egyptologists once thought that Egypt's duality derived from two historical kingdoms, one in Lower and one in Upper Egypt. The union of these two kingdoms would have produced a dual kingdom with a dual 'king of Upper and Lower Egypt'. However, recent archaeology has suggested that no earlier 'kingdom of Lower Egypt' existed; instead, the state of Egypt seems to have grown out of a way of life called the Naqada culture, in Upper Egypt. From c.3500 BC the Naqada culture spread across the entire valley north of the First Cataract, and by c.3000 BC took hold in the Delta. The dual nature of ancient Egypt therefore probably reflects not history but a dualistic view of the world, reinforced by the stark contrast between fields (life) and desert (death). If the world consisted of balanced forces of order and disorder, the king had to embody both in order to exert his control. This image can be seen in two dimensions on the throne of statues of Senusret I where Horus, the god of order, together with Seth, the anarchic god, bind together the plants of Upper and Lower Egypt. The two halves of the kingdom comprise not a kingdom of Upper Egypt and a kingdom of Lower Egypt but the paired opposites in a

Sandstone plaque with the cartouches of
Ramses II. Height 4.1 cm. EA 48664.

perfect unity, the 'Two Lands', the common synonym for 'the Beloved Land'
of Egypt. Likewise, the king is not 'king of Upper and Lower Egypt', but
'dual king' of the dual Egypt.

Those two pillars of kingship, its duality and its limited divinity, permeate
the titles to the five royal names. The first title identifies the king as a form of
the heavenly falcon Horus, god of the sunlit sky of daytime. The Two Ladies
in the second title are the cobra-goddess Wadjet and the vulture-goddess
Nekhbet, later attached respectively to Buto and Elkab, the most northerly
and southerly royal cities of the Early Dynastic kingdom. The Gold in the
third title expresses the divinity of the king, both by its material and its
colour: gold never decays, and thus stands for the flesh of gods and kings, as
eternal beings; in colour and radiance it represents the powerful sunlight of
an Egyptian day. In the fourth title the 'sedge and bee' probably did not
symbolise Upper and Lower Egypt originally; they form a conceptual duality
of uncertain significance in the earlier periods. The first part of the title, 'He
of the Sedge', represents the commonest word for 'king' in Egyptian, perhaps
by abbreviation from the full 'He of the Sedge and Bee'. The fifth title, 'son of
Ra', claims a direct solar origin for the king as child of the sun-god,
summarising in one phrase that Egyptian conception of kingship.

From the Fourth Dynasty on, solar imagery overtook duality in the identity
of the king. In Egyptian texts referring to kingship the word *kha*, 'to rise',
resounds with solar imagery. The word referred not only to the rising of the
sun, but also to the accession of the king and to all appearances of the king,
and even to the insignia he wore at such appearances. That resonance can be
captured at its first instant in an inscription from the reign of Thutmose I.
Turi, viceroy of the southern province of Kush for Thutmose I, recorded on
this inscription the first words addressed to him from the throne by the new
ruler:

Right Sandstone stela of the viceroy Hori, who is shown below adoring the two cartouches of Ramses IV set on the gold sign. Height 1.63 m. EA 66668.

Far right Fragment from a granite statue, with a cartouche containing the throne name of Thutmose I and the epithet 'lord of the strong arm'. Height 40.5 cm. EA 1457.

This royal [decree is brought] to inform you that My Majesty, may he live, prosper and hale, is arisen (*kha*) as He of the Sedge and Bee upon the Horus throne of the living, with no equal in eternity. My titulary has been composed as:

Horus Mighty Bull, Beloved of Truth
He of the Two Ladies, Risen (*kha*) with the fiery serpent, Great of Strength
Horus of Gold, Perfect of Years, He who makes hearts live
He of the Sedge and Bee Aakheperkara
Son of Ra [Thutmose] living forever and eternity

Now you are to have divine offerings presented to the temples of the Southern Reach of Elephantine in doing what is praised upon the life-prosperity-health of He of the Sedge and Bee Aakheperkara given life, and you are to have oaths taken by the name of My Majesty, may he live, prosper and hale, born of the King's Mother Seniseneb, in health. This is sent to inform you on this, and that the Royal Domain flourishes and prospers.

Year 1, month 3 of winter, day 21, day of the feast of the coronation (*kha*).

Thutmose I here proclaims his full titulary as king of Egypt and commands all oaths and temple offerings to be made in his name, setting his fourth titled name, 'He of the Sedge and Bee Aakheperkara', at the heart of the entire religious and judicial structure of the country. In this royal decree can be seen the reasons for the persistent recurrence of royal names throughout the monuments of Egypt. The names underpinned the order of the world by identifying the king at the offerings from man to the gods, and at the oaths of individuals before society. The king, expressed in his names, provides the guarantee of harmony by acting as a lynchpin between heaven and earth.

The grandson of Thutmose I, Thutmose III, explained in one text what each of his names signified when adopted at his 'rising' as king:

[Ra established] my royal risings and conferral of the
titulary upon me himself.
he established my falcon upon the *serekh*-panel and
strengthened me to be mighty bull,
and caused me to rise within Thebes,
[in this my name of Horus Mighty Bull, Risen in Thebes].
[He caused me to raise up the Two Ladies,
and made my kingship last like that of Ra in heaven,
in] this my [name] of He of the Two Ladies, Enduring of
Kingship like Ra in Heaven.
He fashioned me as a falcon of gold,
and gave me his force and his strength;
I was holy in those his divine risings,
in this my name [of Horus of Gold, Powerful in Strength,
Holy in Risings].
[He caused me to rise as He of the Sedge and Bee,
and established my forms as those of Ra
in this my name of] He of the Sedge and Bee, Lord of the
Two Lands, Menkheperra (=established in the forms of Ra).
I am his son who emerged out of him,
the image of birth like the god presiding over Heseret (Thoth)
and he united all my forms
in this my name of Son of Ra Thutmose
United in Form, living forever and
eternity.

The five titled names belong to an intricate language designed both to express the solar character of the reigning king and to reinforce at every moment that king's claim to legitimacy as son of the gods and king of the dual land of Egypt. The explanation of the first four names may lie close to

Painted fragment showing votive falcons for Thutmose III, whose throne name is written between their wings. Deir el-Bahri. Height 7.2 cm. EA 69135.

the original reasons for choosing their particular wording, but the account of the fifth name, Thutmose, reinterprets a common name of the day in the language of kingship. The name itself would have been given at birth before it was certain that he would become king.

The distance between the first four names, compiled at accession, and the fifth name, received at birth, emerges more clearly in a text of the same date, from the royal cult temple of Hatshepsut, daughter of Thutmose I and step-mother to Thutmose III. Hatshepsut violated a first rule of kingship: the sun-god Ra was male, and his emanation, the king, is most easily of the same gender; as a woman, Hatshepsut needed to stress her legitimacy as king, not queen, of Egypt, beyond all the bounds of regular kingship texts. One wall of her temple at Deir el-Bahri bears a record of her divine birth, in which the solar deity takes the guise of the earthly father, Thutmose I, and impregnates the earthly mother. Thoth announces the divine birth to the mother, and the birth is assisted by a host of deities. This wall-scene depicts the regular belief that a king was of solar, not human, seed, but Hatshepsut was the first sovereign to need pictorial proof of the divine birth of the king, to counter doubts that a woman could be intended by heaven as king of Egypt. Alongside, on the same wall, stands the text describing the installation of Hatshepsut as coregent in the lifetime of her father, Thutmose I. The episode may derive from a public display of favour by the king to his daughter, but it permits Hatshepsut to tie her reign to that of her father. Monuments of the time show that the actual course of history was quite different, with a brief reign by her half-brother Thutmose II between Thutmose I and Hatshepsut. By omitting Thutmose II and ignoring the young coregent Thutmose III, Hatshepsut achieves a pure claim for her legitimacy from at once her divine father, the sun, and her earthly father, Thutmose I. In the modified text, Thutmose I informs his courtiers that he installs his daughter as the coregent and future sole king:

His Majesty commanded the lector-priests to
be brought to inscribe her great names of the moment of
receiving her insignia of He of the Sedge and Bee . . .
They then inscribed her names of He of the Sedge and Bee.
Indeed the god inspired their minds to compile her names
exactly as he had compiled them first:
Her great name Horus Powerful in Sustenance
Her great name She of the Two Ladies, Flourishing in
Years, Perfect Goddess and Mistress of Acts,
Her great name Horus of Gold, She the Divine of Risings,
Her great name of He of the Sedge and Bee Maatkara
given life eternally.
That indeed is her true name compiled by the god first.

Only the first four names are compiled by the lector-priests, under the inspiration of the sun-god. The fifth name was already given at birth, and would then be reinterpreted as divine when the person became king.

Hatshepsut took this account of a fictitious coregency with her father from a text describing a genuine coregency of the Middle Kingdom, some three hundred and fifty years earlier. Only fragments of the early text survive, from a temple in the Fayum, but they contain part of the wording of Hatshepsut's text. In the Fayum fragments Senusret III makes his son Amenemhat III coregent and gives him his great names of kingship, inspired by Sobek, crocodile-god of the Fayum and patron of the dynasty. The text is not identical to the Deir el-Bahri version but has been brilliantly adapted to the different circumstances of Hatshepsut.

In her combination of divine birth scene and text of installation by her father, Hatshepsut secures the divine origin of her full identity in all five titled royal names. With this record she could hope to have secured her claim to be not queen but king of Egypt and child of the sun. However, her efforts did not survive her death: her step-son Thutmose III meticulously corrected the record by erasing all traces that a woman had claimed kingship. Only in

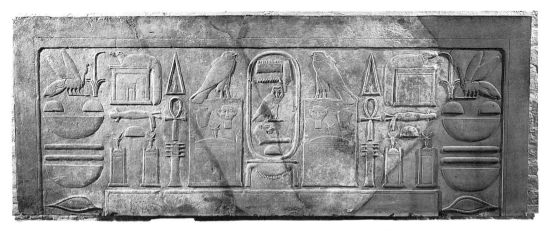

Limestone lintel of Amenemhat III, bearing his cartouche upon the sign for gold, flanked by the names of the gods Horus and Sobek. Length 2.36 m. EA 1072.

Limestone statue of Inebni. The text includes the throne names of Hatshepsut (erased) and Thutmose III. Height 51.5 cm. EA 1131.

modern times have the erased names been read again and the claim of Hatshepsut brought to light.

In addition to these formal royal records there exists one precious manuscript with a series of tales about kingship, including descriptions of divine birth. Papyrus Westcar, named after an associate of the first modern owner, contains a cycle of stories set in the reign of king Khufu of the Fourth Dynasty, builder of the Great Pyramid at Giza. The tales were written down in the sixteenth century BC, and the language would date the text to the Twelfth or Thirteenth Dynasty (c.2000–1650 BC) or about five to nine hundred years after the reign of Khufu. Therefore the contents are roughly rather than precisely historical. The three kings of the line of Khufu correspond in history to the three kings who built pyramids at Giza, while the three kings of the new line in the final tale correspond to the historical group of kings who built royal sun temples as well as pyramids. In the last tale the wife of a priest of Ra in Sakhebu, northwest of the capital city Memphis, has been impregnated by Ra in order to give birth to three divine sons, the first three kings of the Fifth Dynasty. Ra sends Isis with a group of deities to act as midwives for the divine triple birth. At the birth of each child Isis utters a spell to ease the delivery. For the first child she says, 'Do not be forceful in her womb, in this your name of He is Powerful (Egyptian Useref)', echoing the name of the first king of the Fifth Dynasty, Userkaf. The second child receives the address 'Do not tread in her womb, in this your name of Tread of Ra (Egyptian Sahura)', the name of the second king of that dynasty. For the last son Isis utters the words 'Do not darken her womb, in this your name of the Darkener (Egyptian Keku)', echoing the birth name of the third king of the Fifth Dynasty, Keki, or more fully, Kakai. Before leaving earth Isis and her companion deities fashion three 'lordly risings', the evidence for the parents that three future kings have been born to them. Once the deities have gone, the three 'risings' are discovered with loud music and

Serpentine statue of the official Harwa holding two divine female figures with the name of the high priestess Amenirdis, written in a cartouche. Height 17.5 cm. EA 32555.

dances of the kind performed for a king. The 'risings' in this text refer either to crowns or insignia, or even to the festivities of the coronation, or more generally to all the trappings of kingship. Here again, *kha* ('rising' or 'sunrise') denotes the solar and separate essence of kingship, permeating insignia and titulary alike.

Despite the longevity of the fivefold titulary, few moments identify a king by all five titled names. The moment of full naming came at the installation of the king; later, a text would cite the full titulary of the king only to capture the aura of the coronation. Originally the identity of the reigning king lay in his Horus name, but from the Middle Kingdom the fourth name and, to a lesser extent, the fifth came to signify his uniqueness. Towards the end of its history, under the Ptolemies, the titulary no longer held the identity of the reigning king, which was located instead in an external epithet composed in Greek for the foreign, Greek-speaking king. The texts of a period tend to cite only the principal identifying royal name and add other elements of the fivefold titulary only to specific effect. Three of the five names predominate in the texts: the Horus name, particularly before the Middle Kingdom, and then the fourth name (titled 'Sedge and Bee') and the fifth name (birth name).

Basalt block showing king Psamtek I, identified by his Horus name and cartouches. Rosetta (originally Sais?). Height 1.23 m. EA 22.

The writing of the royal titulary highlights the three principal names by using special frames, rectangular for the Horus name and oval for the fourth and fifth names. The Horus name panel depicts the niched façade and rectangular enclosure wall of a palace at the time of the first unification of Egypt (*c.*3000 BC), and is echoed in a later phrase for the king as 'Horus resident in the palace'. This frame was called the *serekh*, literally 'that which makes known', as it proclaimed the name of the king. The oval ring containing the fourth or fifth name of the king grew out of a circle, Egyptian *shen*, echoed in the description of sovereignty as rule over 'all that the sun disc circles'. The oval ring is known in Egyptology as a cartouche, the French word given to it by the first Egyptologists. The cartouche sometimes framed names of people who were not kings, generally queens or princesses, perhaps because their role in the cult of the sun brought them a certain claim to universal recognition on the religious level.

The Horus name panel and the cartouche provide conspicuous means of identifying a king in any text. Kingship stands firmly at the forefront of Egyptian civilisation: even people without any interest in the royal court relied in their prayers on offerings by 'He of the Sedge', the king, to the gods of Egypt, formulated on countless hieroglyphic monuments from the Old Kingdom to the Roman Period as 'an offering given by the king (He of the Sedge)'. The royal names and their development dominate the texts and monuments that have survived. During periods of strong central authority people often named their children after the man on the throne in a display of loyalty, and to secure the divine blessing of an effective king. These loyalist names sometimes contain the throne name of the king, as in Sehetibraankh ('May Sehetepibra (Amenemhat I of the Twelfth Dynasty) live'), and sometimes the birth name, as in Pepyseneb ('May Pepy (name of two kings in the Sixth Dynasty) be well'). Close devotees even kept the cartouche around the royal name within their own. With name apt to replace image, Ramesside officials could depict themselves adoring the royal cartouches. Egyptology itself is a child of the royal names, for the cartouche provided scholars in the late eighteenth and early nineteenth centuries of our era with the key to the lost meaning of the hieroglyphs, a script otherwise devoid of punctuation.

2

The emergence of the fivefold titulary, *c.*3000–2000 BC

At the close of the fourth millennium BC the land from Elephantine to the Delta became a single state ruled by a single man. The new, expanded state also prompted the development of a means of communication and record. The geography of Egypt thus produced at a blow one of the first states and one of the first scripts, and it is no accident that the names of kings appear among the earliest hieroglyphic texts. We cannot reconstruct the exact political events that brought about the unification of Egypt under one ruler, because the texts begin only towards the end of the process. However, from the period immediately preceding unification major tombs, implying concentrations of power, are known at Abydos, Ombos and Hieraconpolis, three towns in Upper Egypt. The tombs at Hieraconpolis and Ombos petered out after unification, but the cemetery at Abydos continued to grow and, thanks to the inscriptions and the quality of surviving burial goods, this cemetery at Abydos can be identified as the first royal necropolis of Egypt. At Saqqara, near the Old Kingdom capital city of Memphis, a series of great tombs bore texts of the same early kings, and these provide the earliest solid evidence that a ruler buried at Abydos controlled the northern end of the Nile Valley as well as Upper Egypt. The Saqqara tombs presumably belonged to governors of the northern province, while the Abydos tombs belonged to the kings themselves.

The first king ruling at both Abydos and Saqqara had the name Aha, or 'fighter'. The name was written on objects in the rectangular panel under the falcon, later identified as Horus over the palace. About two centuries after the

Ivory frangment naming king Aha, with the Horus panel, and a courtier, Imaib. Abydos. Height 3.1 cm. EA 35513.

first falcon panels, two kings used the device with Seth opposite or instead of Horus. Since the falcon-god of order, Horus, and the god of disorder, Seth, formed an opposing pair in later Egytian mythology, the early falcon probably already represents Horus. In Egypt the soaring falcon of the sunlit skies provides a striking image of both royal and celestial power. Before Aha a few falcon panels contain the names of kings, although the script had as yet barely emerged, and many of the texts are difficult to read. The names of a king Scorpion and king Ro do not occur in legible falcon panels, and may be misreadings of more general phrases concerning kingship, for example the presence of the deity in the form of a scorpion to protect the king. Some falcon panels offer a possible royal name Ka, but here, too, there are uncertainties. Later texts identify the falcon Horus as the *ka* ('sustaining spirit') of a king. Possibly the falcon panel with Ka attempts to convey the same idea, that the falcon god is the *ka* of the king, in which case it remains unknown which specific king, which name, lies behind the apparent Ka. The texts of this period abound with difficulties of this nature, because they are the first expressions of the hieroglyphic script and not bound by later rules of use.

In Abydos the first secure royal name before Aha is the king Narmer, whose name was written in the panel under a falcon and can be considered the first certain Horus name. Narmer donated to the already ancient temple of Horus in Heiraconpolis a monumental slate votive palette which shows for the first time a king in possession of both the Red and the White Crown, later symbols of Upper and Lower Egypt. The name Narmer does not occur at

Pottery vessel with a Horus panel containing the sign 'Ka'. Abydos. Height 27 cm. EA 35508.

Saqqara, but it does figure at a slightly more southerly site, Tarkhan. In 1985 German excavations at Abydos uncovered a mud sealing with the imprint of a stone cylinder seal. From the imprint the original seal can be reconstructed, and it evidently bore the Horus names of the first kings in order of rule. As given on the seal, Narmer would be the first king of the group, followed by Aha, Djer, Djet and Den with the 'king's mother Merneit'. From tombs at Abydos we can add at the end of this the first recorded dynasty kings Adjib, Semerkhet and Qa'a.

All eight kings of the First Dynasty were named by the device of the panel surmounted by a falcon. The surviving masterpiece of the age came from the Abydos tomb of Djet, and presents the Horus name in the perfect proportion of classical Egyptian art. Other relics of the tombs do not always match the harmony of the Djet tombstone, but they already contain many of the motifs of later Egyptian kingship. A label of king Den portrays a ritual of enthronement similar to scenes repeated on royal monuments down to the Late Period. The stock royal motifs of the First Dynasty also include elements

Right Ebony label of king Den, marking the *sed* 'kingship festival'. Abydos. Height 5.5 cm. EA 32650.

Below Granite block showing the *sed* festival of Osorkon II (compare the label of Den, above). Height 1.6 m. EA 1105.

of the later fivefold titulary. On a label of king Aha we find the first mention of the Two Ladies, although not as part of a royal name. In the following reign of Djer they recur, this time with the two shrines that came to represent Upper and Lower Egypt. The stela of Djet sums up the energy of the first phase of rule before the next reign, that of king Den, demonstrates a fresh burst of activity. Under Den the royal tomb chamber received a lining of granite blocks, an unprecedented expenditure in manpower for tailoring each slab and moving it the hundreds of miles from the Aswan quarries to Abydos. In the same reign the Horus name is first aligned with the gold-sign, later title of the third royal name in each titulary, and the ring, later elongated for inclusion of the fourth and fifth royal names as the cartouche. The two symbols, gold and ring, in one case stand under a cobra and in another under a vulture, facing the falcon panel that bears the name of the king. Among other innovations of king Den stands the title 'He of the Sedge and Bee', which came to be equivalent to 'king of Egypt', either in the full dual form or in short, 'He of the Sedge'. The Egyptian word for kingship was *nsyt*, derived directly from *nswt*, 'He of the Sedge', and this makes it clear that *nswt* came closest to our word 'king'. Contrary to accepted opinion, there is no evidence that 'He of the Sedge' denoted 'king of Upper Egypt', with 'He of the Bee' denoting 'king of Lower Egypt'. The two terms formed a pair that expressed perfect balance and unity, and the holder of one must hold its partner too.

In the reign of Adjib the title 'He of Sedge and Bee' was set before a second name of the king, Merpabia, but without a ring or cartouche. Throughout this early period the Horus name remained the principal means for identifying the reigning king, while the name with the title 'He of the Sedge and Bee' occurred mostly in secondary contexts such as buildings or ships named after the king. Semerkhet saw one further innovation of the First Dynasty: inclusion of the Two Ladies in the royal titulary. At this early stage the Two Ladies acted not as a title to introduce a separate name, but as part of a name introduced by the title 'He of the Sedge and Bee'. In addition to his falcon panel Semerkhet bore the titled name 'He of the Sedge and Bee Iry-Nebty (meaning 'guard of the Two Ladies')'. The early royal birth names are not known, but they lie behind names given for the period in later kinglists.

At the end of the First Dynasty the elements of the future classic titulary were already in existence, with one all-important exception: a reference to Ra, the sun-god. The first mention of Ra as a god rather than as the word for the sun belongs to the Third Dynasty, and the royal names alone offer an explanation for this development in the names of kingship. A priest called Hetepdief has left to us a statue bearing the falcon panel names of the first three kings of the Second Dynasty. The statue was found at Memphis, implying that the cult of those kings lay nearby. The move of the royal cemetery, and by extension the centre of government, from Abydos to Memphis has been confirmed by the absence of these Second Dynasty kings at Abydos, and by the find of underground passages beneath Third Dynasty royal tombs at Saqqara, the cemetery area of Memphis. However, the last two kings of the Second Dynasty reversed the move to Memphis and were buried instead at Abydos, next to the kings of the First Dynasty. Still more remarkable, one of them, Peribsen, took either in addition to or instead of his

A rare depiction of the god of disorder Seth, adored by the deputy foreman Aapehty. Late Nineteenth Dynasty, *c.* 1200 BC. EA 35630.

falcon panel name a panel name surmounted by the figure of Seth, god of disorder and opposite of Horus. Although kingship combined within itself both the order of Horus and the disorder of Seth, Peribsen alone of all the kings of Egypt chose for his principal name the panel surmounted by Seth.

It is still debated whether the falcon panel name Sekhemib belongs to the same king or to another king immediately preceding him. It is certain, though, that the successor of Peribsen held two panel names, one surmounted by the falcon and reading Khasekhem, 'The Power is Risen', the other surmounted by both falcon and Seth and reading Khasekhemwy, 'The Two Powers are Risen'. From all these variant titles to the panel name it seems clear that the falcon over the panel is Horus as the opposite of Seth. The changing titles and burial places may have created an imbalance in the perfect formula that the king is Horus and Seth, and any uncertainty may have promoted belief in one overriding power, set above the dualism of creation, order and disorder. The second king of the Second Dynasty held the name Nebra, which probably means 'lord of the sun', but the position is reversed in the Third Dynasty when we find an official called not after the king but after the sun-god, with the name Hesyra, 'praised by Ra'. In place of the perfectly but precariously balanced opposites Horus and Seth, the king would stand under a new and undisputed heavenly force, Ra the sun-god. In the following dynasties Seth no longer competes with the falcon of Horus on the royal name panel, while Ra grows steadily in importance among the royal names. Parallel to the rise of Ra in texts, the royal tomb itself becomes that purest solar form, the pyramid.

The Third Dynasty returned decisively to Memphis, and there on the desert edge at Saqqara the minister Imhotep surpervised the inspired creation of the earliest pyramid, the Step Pyramid, to house the body of his king, Djoser. Like the monument, the names of Djoser remain rooted in the Early Dynastic, with varying combinations of the gold-sign, the ring and the title 'He of the Sedge and Bee' with the Two Ladies. Only in the reign of king Sneferu of the Fourth Dynasty do we find, with the true pyramid, the use of a new device, the elongated ring or cartouche to hold a second name of the king. Henceforth all kings were known more by their cartouche name than by their Horus name: Sneferu, for example, is the ringed cartouche name of the king whose Horus name was Nebmaat. The importance of the new cartouche name may account for its inclusion in a falcon panel alongside the Horus name as early as the reign of Khafra in the Fourth Dynasty. Sneferu also combined for the first time the gold-sign with the falcon. Khufu, Khafra and Menkaura, kings of the Giza Pyramids, were able to build on the forms established by king Sneferu, and Khafra joined to the falcon and gold-sign an extra sign to make the titled name 'the Gold, Horus the powerful', prototype for third names in the classic titulary of later years. However, the son of Khufu who did not build at Giza, king Djedefra, was the king who brought Ra to the royal titulary at a more fundamental level. His cartouche name includes the name of Ra and means 'Ra is his strength'. With few exceptions, subsequent kings of Egypt included Ra in their throne name, indicating the new centre of gravity in Egyptian belief. Furthermore, Djedefra was the first king to use the phrase 'son of Ra' in his titulary. In the course of the Old Kingdom the phrase 'son of Ra' was to evolve from this epithet into a fixed title for one of the five names of the king.

In the Fifth Dynasty the kings held varying titled names, in which the elements 'Two Ladies', 'Gold' and 'He of the Sedge and Bee' figured. The fixed elements in this emerging titulary were the horus name and the

Broken votive falcon in anhydrite, with the cartouche of Sneferu, from his posthumous cult at Serabit el-Khadim in Sinai. Middle Kingdom. Height 13 cm. EA 41745.

The cartouches of Menkaura and
Shepseskaf, cited in the biography of
a high official Ptahshepses.
EA 682 (detail).

cartouche names. Each Horus name was unique to that king, as was each cartouche name. In the reign of Neferirkara, third king of the Fifth Dynasty, the king bears for the first time two cartouche names. A first name, in that case Neferirkara, was used on monuments during the lifetime of the king. A second name written in a cartouche appeared only after the death of the king, in the first case Kakai. Unlike the first name, which always closed with the name Ra, the second cartouche name tended not to contain Ra at all. This second name seems to have been less sacred than the name which Ra used in the king's lifetime, and is thought to have been the name given to the king at birth. The first cartouche name would then have been a replacement pronounced with the Horus name at enthronement. For this reason Egyptologists tend to call the first cartouche the throne name and the second cartouche the birth name.

For all the kings before Neferirkara Kakai we cannot be sure that the cartouche gives the original birth name rather than a new name taken at accession, a throne name. From the moment when two cartouches appear, however, one of them contains the birth name given to the king when he emerged from the womb. In the Sixth Dynasty the birth name was no longer suppressed during the reign of the king, and the pattern of royal names was set for the following two and a half thousand years. The Horus name and the two cartouches were pre-eminent, but the full titulary included the Two Ladies and the Gold elements. Only the separation of names and titles, and the classic order remained to be fixed. One Sixth Dynasty ruler offers a last lesson from the Pyramid Age. His birth name, Pepy, is preceded by the title 'son of Ra' inside the cartouche, as was usual in the Old Kingdom. However, his throne name in cartouche was variable: on some monuments he is Meryra Pepy, on others he is Nefersahor Pepy, whereas his Horus name remains Merytawy. In other words, the king could be identified by his unchanging Horus name more quickly than by his variable throne name or his common birth name. When his birth name is used to identify him a Roman numeral must be added to distinguish him from the later Pepy II – otherwise, at most periods of Egyptian history a single name could identify a king among the royal pantheon. The names of Pepy I demonstrate that still at the end of the Old Kingdom that unique name was the Horus name, as it had been at the beginning of the kingdom.

The Old Kingdom fell apart after the Sixth Dynasty in the tensions between the central government and the ambitions of provincial families. The Eighth Dynasty maintained a semblance of royal authority, but texts indicate growing independence in Upper Egypt. Finally, the kingdom was split outright between a northern king from Heracleopolis in Middle Egypt and a southern king at Thebes, the new city of Upper Egypt. In the struggle for domination the titulary underwent some revision on both sides. The Heracleopolitan king Meryibra Khety set the phrase 'son of Ra' outside the cartouche for his birth name, a title that lasted to the close of Pharaonic history. A more fundamental shift occurred among the titled names of the Theban kings in the south. We have seen that the Horus name of the Old Kingdom did not change once chosen for a reign and that it stands out as the prime name of the king. However, the Theban ruler Nebhepetra Mentuhotep, who achieved victory over the Heracleopolitans and reunited Egypt for a new era of unity, the Middle Kingdom, changed his Horus name twice on the path to reunification (although he left both his cartouche names untouched: throne name Nebhepetra and birth name Mentuhotep). At this critical moment in Egyptian history we see the main shift in the meaning of the royal names. The king is no longer first an incarnation of Horus, with a pre-eminent and unchanging Horus name; he has become first and foremost the king ('He of the Sedge and Bee'), and son of the sun-god ('son of Ra'). The cartouches take over as the vessel for the identity of the king, and the Horus name, though placed first, ranks third in the order of the titulary.

3

The classic titulary, c.2000–1300 BC

The Eleventh Dynasty, the Theban kings who achieved reunification
c.2000 BC, gave way to the Twelfth Dynasty, a family of some of the most
powerful kings in Egyptian history. The first king of the new family was
Amenemhat I who moved the royal Residence to Itj-tawy, south of the Old
Kingdom capital city Memphis. His titulary changed once early in his reign,
giving new Horus, Two Ladies and Gold names but leaving both his throne
name Sehetepibra and his birth name Amenemhat untouched. The change in
his titulary confirms that the cartouche names were now the central hallmark
of each king's distinctive identity, while the Horus name had become a
variable. By implication, the identity of a king no longer lay in his role as
incarnation of Horus: although that continued to play a crucial role in
legitimatising the king, his identity was expressed foremost in his title as
ruler of a double land, 'He of the Sedge and Bee', and in his title as offspring
of the sun-god, 'son of Ra'. The son of Amenemhat I, Senusret I, set up
monumental Horus names at the borders of his pyramid complex near
modern Lisht, and on these he combined the name belonging to his Horus
panel with one or other of his cartouche names, as if the Horus name alone
no longer sufficed to secure his identification as king. The combination of
Horus name and cartouche name in a falcon panel echoes the earlier case of
Khafra described above (p. 25). The new order of importance did not
completely oust the Horus name, which replaces the image of the king on
one royal stela of Senusret I, on which the cartouche names are replaced by
regal epithets. Yet the Horus name ceded ground to the cartouches when the
Twelfth Dynasty brought the five titled names into their final, classic order.

The fourth king of the line, Senusret II, held a Two Ladies name in which
for the first time the Two Ladies cannot be part of the name and must then be
a title. Some have interpreted the title 'Two Ladies' as evidence that the king
was identified as an earthly form of the two goddesses, Wadjyt and Nekhbet,
but it seems more likely that the writing *Nebty*, 'Two Ladies', conceals an
additional y at the end and that the title should really read *Nebtyy*, 'He of the
Two Ladies'. The titled name 'He of the Two Ladies' sets the king under the
protection of the two tutelary goddesses of the Two Lands, as portrayed in
scenes of kingship.

The classic series for the five titled names established by the Twelfth
Dynasty was as follows: Horus name, Two Ladies name, Gold name, throne
name (in a cartouche) and birth name (in a cartouche). This arrangement
appears in both royal and non-royal or 'private' texts. In existing sources the

Reconstructed *serekh*-panel from the pyramid enclosure wall of Senusret I, with the Horus
name and one cartouche name of the king. Photograph courtesy of the Metropolitan
Museum of Art, New York.

Stela recording a decree of Senusret III. The Horus and throne names of the king face the god Horus son of Isis. Height 75 cm. EA 852.

full five names do not often occur together: even a decree of king Senusret III gives only his Horus name and one cartouche. In one very lengthy inscription, at Beni Hasan in Middle Egypt, the local governor Khnumhotep refers to his king sometimes by the full titulary, sometimes by the cartouche names only. From the contents of the text it can be shown that the full titulary served to reinforce in the strongest way possible the governor's loyal service of a glorious ruler. At less strategic points in the text the governor evidently felt no need to invoke the full aura of the titulary, and to identify the king he needed only the throne name. The aura surrounding the full titulary can be explained by the Fayum text mentioned in Chapter 1 (p. 15), where the crocodile-god Sobek inspires the naming of the king. This gave every recitation of the five names not only the resonance of the great festivals of kingship, but also a direct link with the gods. Royal titularies are found upon private monuments perhaps partly for this reason.

After the prosperity of the Twelfth Dynasty Egypt lost her single ruling family and found no replacement, although the short-reigned kings who succeeded the Twelfth Dynasty continued to rule from Itj-tawy and upheld every tradition of the preceding age. However, the new group of kings, known today as the Thirteenth Dynasty, brought no new life to the country: their names indicate a reverence for the past, and the most frequent form of

Left Base of a statue of Khaankhra Sobekhotep with his cartouches. Height 13.5 cm. EA 69497.

Below (top) Blue-glazed steatite scarab of Khyan in its gold mount. Length 3.2 cm. EA 37664; (bottom) Lapis lazuli scarab of a king Intef, set in gold. Length 1.6 cm. EA 57698.

identification continued to lie in the two cartouches, for throne name and birth name. The fivefold titulary was consolidated at this time, and the Gold name now took the falcon as a constant part of the title, to read 'Horus of Gold'. When the population of Palestine spilt over into the Eastern Nile Delta in the eighteenth century BC none of the Thirteenth Dynasty kings at Itj-tawy could stem the tide. During the later years of the eighteenth century BC this part of the Delta split off from the kingdom under a prince called Nehesy and his successors, the group we term the Fourteenth Dynasty. The secession of the Eastern Delta provided a platform for foreign power: in *c.*1650 BC the settlers there took hold of the north of Egypt with rulers known to us as Hyksos, a Greek version of Egyptian *heqa khasut* ('rulers of foreign lands'). The main foreign rulers ruled from Avaris in the Eastern Delta, and form the Fifteenth Dynasty of Manetho. A number of lesser foreign rulers are known to us as the Sixteenth Dynasty, while the indigenous rulers were restricted to a smaller kingdom based at Thebes, as the Seventeenth Dynasty.

Remarkably, the foreign rulers copied local practice in royal names. They took two cartouche names, one a throne name with reference to Ra, the other their own foreign birth name. They did not apparently use the other three titled names for the titulary, and later an Egyptian scribe compiling a kinglist wrote their royal names without cartouches, as if to deny their claim to sovereignty. At Thebes the Seventeenth Dynasty retained the heritage of the past with full titularies. After decades of coexistence the rival Hyksos and Theban dynasties came to blows. Dispute began under the Theban king Seqenenra Taa, who seems to have founded a new royal Residence at a site near Dendera, Deir el-Ballas. His skull has survived and bears the imprint of an axe-type used by the northern foreigners. His successor, Kamose, continued the fight and laid siege to Avaris itself, but he died after a short reign; the expulsion of the Hyksos was then left to the next ruler, Ahmose I, who moved from the royal Residence at Deir el-Ballas shortly after his final victory, its strategic position no longer so vital. The wars continued outside Egypt, south and north, to prevent a repeat of Hyksos rule. The reunification of Egypt inaugurated the New Kingdom, an age marked by the spirit of the wars in which it was born.

Ahmose I was the first of a group of kings known to us as the Eighteenth Dynasty. The third king of this group, apparently unrelated to Ahmose I or his family, was Thutmose I, who embarked on military ventures deep into foreign lands north and south of Egypt, and took in his Horus name the

epithet 'Mighty Bull'. Cartouche names also received supplementary epithets in some cases, and these came eventually to play a decisive role in identifying the king. Except for queen Hatshepsut and the heretic king Akhenaten, every ruler until the Kushite period added the epithet 'Mighty Bull' to his Horus name, reflecting the martial flavour of the times. The two exceptions demonstrate the military significance of the 'Mighty Bull' in the Horus name. Hatshepsut undertook campaigns, but she chose not to highlight them in her cult temple at Deir el-Bahri. As a female ruler claiming to be rightful king of Egypt, she fell foul of posterity and her monuments were carefully censored during the ensuing years. Any representation of Hatshepsut as a sovereign and any text giving her the titles and epithets of kingship were chiselled neatly out of existence. The Egyptians regarded two- and three-dimensional representation as real substitutes for flesh-and-blood existence, and an image or text secured for the subject eternal life in the status portrayed. Conversely, erasing a text or image sufficed to destroy its power to give the subject life or, in the case of Hatshepsut, royal status.

Whereas Hatshepsut was to be denied the status of king, Akhenaten is unique among Egyptian kings for the destruction of not only his name but also his city and his god. Akhenaten came to the throne towards the end of the Eighteenth Dynasty as Amenhotep IV. He focused his attention on worshipping the sun-god, and erected beside the temple of the state god Amun at Karnak a temple for the sun in the form Ra-Horakhty ('Ra perceived through Horus-of-the-horizon', in other words the sun at dawn). Five years after becoming king he departed on a radical path, the greatest upheaval in the history of ancient Egyptian religion: he abandoned the old gods and cities and founded a new city dedicated to the sun, not in the form of invisible deity expressed in human and animal symbolism, but in the form of the visible sun disc, Aton in the Egyptian language. Startlingly, the god was to receive two cartouches and uraeus-snakes, exactly like a king. The name of the god was formulated in the two cartouches as 'Ra Horakhty jubilant in the horizon, in his name as Shu (daylight) who is in the Aton (sun disc)'. Even the mention of other gods to describe him became impermissible, leading to a new formulation of the name as 'the sun, the ruler of the horizon, jubilant in the horizon, in his name as the light which comes from the Aton'. The king went one step further in his love of the Aton and changed his name from Amenhotep, meaning 'Amun is content', to Akhenaten, 'beneficial to the Aton'. He banned the god Amun, and sent out teams of agents to destroy the name of Amun wherever they could find it, deep into the southern provinces, at the height of every obelisk, even in the names of Akhenaten's predecessors (removing 'Amen' from Amenhotep, for example). The model for his actions may have been the erasure of Hatshepsut's kingship, but the iconoclasm against Amun was on a much grander scale.

In the wake of Akhenaten's death the pendulum swung as hard against him and harder. The boy king Tutankhamun returned to the city of Memphis to carry out a programme of restoration, continued by his successors Ay and Horemheb. However Tutankhamun, perhaps a son of

Ivory ring with a faience scarab of Akhenaten, named by his throne name and its standard epithet 'sole one of Ra'. Diameter 2.5 cm. EA 54578.

Rough limestone block of king Horemheb. Amarna. Height 10 cm. EA 58468.

Akhenaten, and Ay, a member of Akhenaten's court, were both tainted with the mark of heresy. So Horemheb destroyed their names, too, and took for his own a series of the restoration monuments of the two kings. Religious policy may have been instrumental in Horemheb's activity of usurping earlier monuments, yet it set a precedent that was energetically taken up by later kings. The cost of recutting names was incomparably less than that of commissioning new stone monuments from the desert quarries and transporting them to a temple already filled with the work of previous kings.

In one important reform Akhenaten succeeded: he introduced the use of Late Egyptian, the spoken language of the New Kingdom, for royal monuments. In the Eighteenth Dynasty the official language had been Middle Egyptian after the classic model of the Twelfth Dynasty; between the Middle and New Kingdoms it had changed from a synthetic to an analytic form of the same language, equivalent to the shift from Anglo-Saxon to modern English. After Akhenaten either the outdated classic form or the spoken everyday language could be used in texts. For general reference to the king in the Middle Kingdom the word *neb* ('Lord') was used, which also applied to gods and superiors at work. The appearance of Late Egyptian in the texts brought a new term to refer uniquely to the king, *per 'aa* ('the Great House'), an expression that had previously denoted the palace but not directly the king. The Hebrew version of *per 'aa* in the Bible gives us our word Pharaoh. This new tolerance in the official language affected the royal names at their root, encouraging the growth of continuous phrases and epithets to replace the concise formulas of the Old and Middle Kingdoms. A title of Horemheb echoes precedents but may presage this development: 'He of the Sedge and Bee, the ruler of the nine bows, lord of the two lands, Djeserkheperura chosen by Ra'.

With the Nineteenth Dynasty the classic simplicity of the titulary gave way almost entirely to the prestige of Egypt's greatest builder king, Ramses II.

4

Variations: the elaborate and the pure, *c*.1300–30 BC

After the death of Horemheb a new family came to power, the Nineteenth Dynasty. Its first king, Ramses I, ruled probably little more than a year, but his son, Sety I, and grandson, Ramses II, gave Egypt some of her most splendid edifices, notably the two royal cult temples at Abydos and the Hypostyle Hall in the temple of Amun at Karnak. While the monuments of Sety I belong to the outstanding achievements of art in Egypt, it seems clear that Ramses II had his eye on quantity. Statues of Ramses II loomed at virtually every major temple in the land, each adorned with his cartouches. Existing statues were often renamed in his honour, to be housed in his new

Left Votive falcon of Ramses II. Tell el-Maskhuta. Height 95 cm. EA 1006.

Above right Watercolour by Henry Salt of a scene in the tomb of Sety (written Osiry) I at Thebes, drawn in *c*. 1818. EA without number.

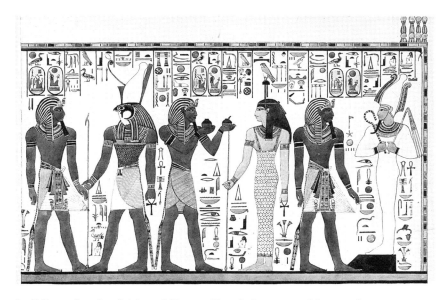

buildings for the deities of Egypt. For their vast architectural programmes both Sety I and Ramses II devised a wide repertoire of titled names and epithets, among which only the basic cartouche names remained constant. The number of titled names seems at first glance anarchic, but each change in name and epithet corresponds to the location of the name on the particular site: for example, in the Hypostyle Hall at Karnak the epithet 'beloved of the god Ptah' occurs only on the route to the small sanctuary of Ptah north of the main Amun temple. The epithet here picks out the route taken by the circulation of offerings from the main to the subsidiary temple. In more obvious cases the epithet or name reflects the locality, so that one might expect to find 'beloved of the god Thoth' at his cult centre in Ashmunein. A curious effect of place on name can be seen in the Osirian monuments of Sety I. Osiris, god of the dead, was murdered by his brother, the god of chaos Seth, and the name Sety itself means 'He of Seth'. In order to avoid the name of Seth in the shrines of his victim, the Egyptians there wrote the name Sety not with the hieroglyph for Seth but instead with a sign representing the sacred knot of Isis with the sound value *tit* or *set*.

Ramses II reigned for sixty-six years, and left his mark on every corner of the realm. For the next four centuries Egyptian kings lived in his shadow, and this is nowhere more clearly seen than in the titled names of his successors. The throne name of Ramses II was Usermaatra, with the stock epithet 'chosen by Ra'. The throne name found an echo in Greek as Ozymandias, the king whose folly of arrogance Shelley sought to convey in his poem. Closer in time to Ramses II, both cartouche names Usermaatra and Ramses found a chorus of echoes in the royal names of the Nineteenth and Twentieth Dynasties: even a king of the stature of Ramses III, in the Twentieth Dynasty, adopted the throne name Usermaatra and distinguished himself from Ramses II only by a different choice of epithet, 'beloved of Amun' instead of 'chosen by Ra'. After Ramses III a further eight kings in a row held the birth name Ramses. During the reign of the last Ramses, eleventh

Above left Granite gateway block showing Osorkon II and queen Karoma. Bubastis. Height 1.75 m. EA 1077.

Above right Quartzite *shabti* of Taharqo. Nuri. Height 51 cm. EA 55485.

of that name, the powers behind the throne reached a new settlement by which northern Egypt was ruled by a king at Tanis, and Thebes with Upper Egypt was left to Theban authorities, the highest of whom took the position of High Priest of Amun. Ramses XI apparently lived out his days as king in Piramses, the capital city built in the Delta by Ramses II. In these closing years of the Twentieth Dynasty Egypt lost her foreign provinces and the two ruling groups of this disunited age looked back to the New Kingdom for confirmation of their power. In their tangle of names and epithets a reference to some legitimatising predecessor replaced the desire to retain a separate identity, and so today the precise order and identity of these kings is often disputed.

Some innovations were made during this Intermediate Period, such as the use of the White Crown as an element of the throne name of Nesbanebdjed. On the whole the names repeat one another in detail, and the arrival of Libyan rulers, the Twenty-Second Dynasty, brought only temporary respite before the elaboration of existing names continued. The Libyans imposed unity for some decades, and effectively renewed kingship traditions from antiquity. Yet eventually the country broke up again, this time into a fragmented patchwork of small states. The splintered sovereignty of the land rediscovered its unity only through external forces: in the midst of the divisions of the eighth century BC the Kushite king Piankhi led an army out of what is now the Sudan to force the local dynasts in Egypt to accept a single Pharaoh. To commemorate his triumph Piankhi set up a great stela bearing a vividly detailed account of the campaign, down to the royal lament that horses had starved in the siege of a city. Through Piankhi's action the Kushite rulers became kings of Egypt, as her Twenty-Fifth Dynasty. The birth names of Piankhi's successors are Meroitic, the language of Kush: Shabako, Shabitko, Taharqo and Tanutamani. However, their throne names revert to a classic form not often seen in Egypt since the Eighteenth Dynasty: Neferkara, Djedkara, Nefertumkhura and Bakara. Unlike the Hyksos, the Kushite rulers retained all five titled names of Pharaoh, reflecting their respect for tradition combined with their renewal of Egyptian art.

Kushite rule ended abruptly with the Assyrian invasions of Egypt in 671, 667 and 664 BC. The Assyrians left the government of Egypt to a local family in Sais, and increasing domestic difficulties kept the Assyrians off the Egyptian front long enough to allow their supposed governor in Sais to emerge as king of Egypt and founder of a new line, the Twenty-Sixth Dynasty. The new kings presided over the fourth and last of the classic periods in Egyptian history, known as the Late Period. The foundations for the renewed greatness of Egypt lay in the period of Kushite rule, so that the Twenty-Fifth Dynasty is often now included within the term Late Period. Indeed, the development of art carried directly on from Kushite classicism, and the same can be seen in the names of the kings. All the throne names of the Twenty-Sixth Dynasty end -ibra, echoing the simplicity of Kushite throne names and identifying the king with the same ease. Nevertheless, the kings from Sais did not regard themselves as successors to the Kushites, whose own descendants continued to rule in Kush itself. Relations broke

Alabaster canopic jar of general Neferibraemakhet. The name of the general and his father, Psamteksineit, incorporate the cartouches of their kings. EA 36626.

down entirely in the reign of Psamtek II, who led an army against the Kushite capital Napata, and in the same reign the names of Kushite rulers were expunged from the official record. The Meroitic name seems to have offended the Egyptians particularly, because it was removed from cartouches even when the Egyptian names of a Kushite king were left intact.

The Twenty-Sixth Dynasty itself fell to invasion, this time from the new Near Eastern superpower, Achaemenid Persia. The invasion met with a continual series of rebellions, often backed by men, arms and money from the rising Greek city states. These brought grim retribution, which in turn earned the Persians the unenviable reputation of rulers of unparalleled cruelty. In fact, some Persian kings at least accepted the local tradition of kingship and adopted hieroglyphic titularies, and they are accordingly included in the kinglist of Manetho as the Twenty-Seventh Dynasty. First of the Persian conquerors, Cambyses even employed a priest at Sais in an exemplary renewal of the temple of the goddess Neith, the very patron deity of the defeated Twenty-Sixth Dynasty. The priest, named Wedjahorresnet, commissioned a magnificent statue upon which he recorded the highlights of his career, including the 'making of the titulary' for Cambyses. None of the Persian kings actually left a full titulary, but Cambyses had his Persian name written in a cartouche and Wedjahorresnet devised for him the Egyptian throne name Mesutira. The king also took as his Horus name the evocative phrase Sematawy, 'Unifier of the Two Lands'. In the reign of Cambyses' successor, Darius I, a temple in Egyptian style at Kharga oasis was finished and decorated in the name of the Persian king. In the course of his reign Darius employed two different Horus names and three throne names. No other Persian king held an Egyptian name, but at least three others had their Persian name written in a cartouche. Rebel Egyptian rulers are sometimes known only from Greek sources, such as the prince Inarus whose decade of revolt ended in his capture and execution. The Egyptian names, where known, suggest that rebels did not take the five titled names until they controlled the entire land, in other words until their rebellion met with success. This occurred in 402 BC when a king, Amyrtaeus, expelled the Persians with the help of Sparta. Until the next Persian invasion in 342 BC Delta princes were free to compete for the throne of Egypt.

The Twenty-Eighth Dynasty consists solely of the Saite ruler Amyrtaeus, who was taken to Mendes and murdered there by a rival, Nefaarud (in Greek Nepherites). Nefaarud became founder of the Twenty-Ninth Dynasty, from Mendes. Under one of his successors 'Nepherites II', a certain general Nakhtnebef (in Greek Nectanebo) of Sebennytos, yet another Delta city, rebelled and took the throne for his own line. Despite the internecine bloodshed and the threat of invasion from Persia, these last Egyptian Pharaohs brought back the splendour of lost ages. They took all five titled names, and we can deduce from this that they conducted full traditional ceremonies of enthronement. A renewel of ancient names recalled for Nefaarud I the achievements of the Ramessides, through the throne name Baenra, used by Merenptah, son and successor of Ramses II; Nakhtnebef evoked the glory of Senusret I, through their shared throne name Kheperkara. The continuity of

Statue of Wedjahorresnet, inscribed with his biography. Photograph courtesy of the Vatican Museums.

Basalt slab of Psamtek I, carved on the reverse by Nakhtnebef (Nectanebo I) whose Horus name and cartouches are nourished by the cobra-goddess Wadjyt. Rosetta (originally Sais?) Height 1.23 m. EA 22.

their line was shattered by defeat at the hands of Artaxerxes III, whose revenge for sixty years of Egyptian independence allegedly included killing the sacred ram of Mendes. No hieroglyphic writing of Artaxerxes III is attested.

Rebellion upon the murder of Artaxerxes III failed to gain for Egypt freedom from Persia, and she had to wait for another foreigner, the Macedonian Alexander the Great. Like the first Persian conqueror, Alexander took a Horus name and throne name in addition to a cartouche with his own birth name written in Egyptian. His first Horus name proclaimed him as 'Protector of Egypt', and his throne name, Meryamun Setepenra, 'Beloved of Amun, Chosen by Ra', cast back to epithets of the Ramesside hero kings. The successor of Alexander, Philip Arrhidaeus, held a full titulary with all five titled names, as did the boy king Alexander IV of Macedon. The Horus name of Alexander IV took the element *hun* ('youth'), a point taken up by most of the Ptolemies as if claiming legitimacy not only from the god of kingship, Horus-son-of-Isis, but also from the last heir to the legacy of Alexander the Great.

In 305/4 BC the Macedonian governor of Egypt, Ptolemy, son of Lagus and Cleopatra (three centuries before the famous queen), took the throne of Egypt for himself. He held four of the five titled names of the ancient titulary, and his successors maintained the full series down to Ptolemy XII, last ruler before the arrival of the Romans. The decree stones set up under Ptolemy III, IV and V even have interpretations for the old hieroglyphic titulary in the terms of the third and second centuries BC, with demotic and Greek offering the following 'translations' of the titles:

Horus	'king'
Two Ladies	'lord of diadems'
Horus of Gold	'Master of his Foes'
He of Sedge and Bee	'king of the upper and lower regions'

However, the Pharaonic titulary could not effectively identify a Ptolemy because the family was Macedonian and spoke only Greek. The capital city was not an ancient Egyptian centre but Alexandria, the foundation of Alexander the Great, and the language of the court was Greek. Consequently the king held first and foremost his Macedonian name, Ptolemy, and a Greek epithet that stood outside the fivefold titulary. These, then, were the dying days of a tradition first visible in the First Dynasty. Ptolemy I called himself Soter, 'the Saviour', a word that coincided neatly with Egyptian *sote*, 'to save'. Later Ptolemies required more than one epithet to mark out their own distinctive identity: Ptolemy XII added to his name four epithets (Neos, Dionysius, Philopator, Philadelphus), of which only one (Dionysius) had not been used by previous Ptolemies.

The queens of the line stood more fully in Egyptian tradition. Their names were often written in the cartouche, symbol of sovereignty, and their

Limestone stela showing Ptolemy VII and two of the Cleopatras before the deities Amun, Mut and Khonsu of Thebes. Height 62 cm. EA 612.

Sandstone stela recording repaired flood damage under Tiberius, who is shown before Mut and Khonsu in Egyptian style. Height 66.3 cm. EA 398.

posthumous cults attracted a following from the indigenous population, reflected in the three Macedonian names for Egyptian women: Arsinoe, Berenice and Cleopatra. The last Cleopatra stood true to the formidable tradition of three centuries in Ptolemaic queenly power. Her ambitions reached out over the entire Graeco-Roman world, but her defeat by Octavian, the future emperor Augustus, brought about her suicide and the end of the Ptolemaic dynasty in 30 BC. It may be noted that this Cleopatra, seventh queen of the name, did not claim to be king of Egypt as Hatshepsut had done. She did not take the five titled names, and her Horus name and cartouches followed precedents set by an earlier Ptolemaic queen, Berenice II.

The Roman emperors regarded Egypt as their personal domain, a unique land among the provinces of the Empire. Like the Ptolemies and Persians before them, they built temples for Egyptian gods in Egyptian style, and had

Sandstone stela with empty cartouches. Height 76.2 cm. EA 1325.

their Roman names written in hieroglyphs and Egyptian names devised. Yet the fivefold titulary was never reinstated. The Julio-Claudian emperors took a Horus name, but thereafter even that once pre-eminent name was given only to Titus, Domitian and Antoninus Pius. A cartouche possibly reading Diocletian closes the history of the names of Pharaoh in Egypt. Far to the south in the distant land of Kush, Meroitic kings maintained the tradition of the cartouches but not of the full fivefold titulary. For fifteen centuries the hieroglyphs lost their meaning and the monuments stood mute, until Champollion was able to combine accepted readings of Ptolemaic cartouches with his own reading of the cartouche Ramses, and the hieroglyphs could again be read. In the wake of that decipherment the German scholar Lepsius led a royal expedition to Egypt. At the top of the Great Pyramid Lepsius composed a hieroglyphic text for his royal benefactor, including a cartouche for the royal name, a close echo of a tradition that endured three thousand years, but that had been dead for fifteen centuries.

5

Principal names of the kings of Egypt

Except for the First to Third Dynasties and the early Eleventh Dynasty, the cartouches presented the main one or two names of the king. Before the development of the cartouche in the Fourth Dynasty the Horus name stood out as the only framed royal name. The kings of the early Eleventh Dynasty controlled only the Theban region, and each took only a Horus name beside the cartouche for the birth name. Therefore the following list cites all the major rulers, together with a selection of less important kings, by their cartouches, apart from First to Third Dynasty kings, cited by Horus name, and the early Eleventh Dynasty kings who are cited by Horus name and cartouche. Whenever more than one cartouche is given for a king, the throne name is placed uppermost in this list, and distinguished in the English form by a T. The other cartouches hold the birth names of the kings. Any readers of hieroglyphs should remember that the Egyptians wrote the names of gods at the start of a personal name, regardless of pronunciation, as a mark of reverence. Epithets added to birth names are given in parentheses after the birth name itself in my English versions. I include the reasons for grouping each set of kings as a separate dynasty, and note any major events or developments in the appropriate reigns. The dates given for each group of kings are approximate calculations from the ancient kinglists, the extracts from Manetho and contemporary documents, and they are the subject of continuing debate and research.

First Dynasty, c.3100–2890 BC

These eight kings presided over the first united Egyptian state and the emergence of the hieroglyphic script. From this beginning to the end of the indigenous dynasties, kingship, script, art and religion interlocked in the historic fusion that we call Pharaonic civilisation. The tombs of the First Dynasty kings lie in a confined section of the cemeteries at Abydos.

NARMER

Named on the necropolis seal of Den as first ruler of the First Dynasty. His position seems confirmed by the famous votive palette on which he is shown wearing both the crowns of dual Egypt.

Ivory fragment with the panel name Nar, short for Narmer. Naqada. Height 3.5 cm. EA 55587.

AHA

First king under whom a governor built a tomb at Saqqara, the cemetery of Memphis. Aha may then have been the founder of Memphis, the city which came to be the capital of Egypt in the Old Kingdom (Third to Eighth Dynasties).

DJER

The earliest surviving royal jewellery comes from an arm found in the tomb of Djer. In the Middle Kingdom and afterwards the Egyptians thought that this tomb housed the body of Osiris, god of the dead. The king left an inscription near Wadi Halfa, evidence for a military campaign deep into Nubia.

DJET

DEN

Den was buried in a chamber lined with costly granite from Aswan, which marks the reign as a time of prosperity and royal initiative. He was the first king to hold the title *nswt bity* ('He of the Sedge and Bee') or 'dual king'.

ADJIB

SEMERKHET

QAA

Second Dynasty, *c.*2890–2686 BC

The first three kings of the dynasty were probably buried in tombs at Saqqara, surviving only as underground corridors beneath the royal tombs of the Third Dynasty.

The last two kings of the dynasty were buried at Abydos. Peribsen took a panel name with Seth instead of Horus; the Horus name Sekhemib is either the second name of Peribsen, or a separate king not buried at Abydos. The last king took both a Horus name, Khasekhem, and a panel name with both Horus and Seth, Khasekhmwy. He deposited votive objects at the Horus temple in Hieraconpolis, including the earliest surviving royal sculpture in stone. The great mudbrick panelled enclosures at Abydos and Hieraconpolis may represent royal cult centres of this ruler.

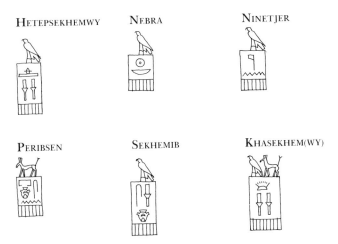

Third Dynasty, c.2686–2613 BC

An uncertain number of kings, buried at Saqqara. Here king Netjerikhet built the Step Pyramid to house his body and achieve immortality, and around it stood life-size stone copies of royal cult buildings. New Kingdom visitors left graffiti in which the king of the pyramid has the cartouche Djoser, now thought to be the birth name of Netjerikhet. The king's First Minister, Imhotep, was credited with the design, the model for all later pyramids, and he became a god of science of the Late Period. The tomb of king Sekhemkhet also took the form of a Step Pyramid, but was never completed. Kings of the Third Dynasty sent expeditions to Sinai to procure turquoise, malachite and copper.

Fourth Dynasty, c.2613–2494 BC

The rulers of the Old Kingdom (Fourth to Eighth Dynasties) cannot yet be grouped on secure historical grounds. The sole papyrus kinglist, from the reign of Ramses II, gives no break at all between the First and Eighth

Dynasties, and the groupings by Manetho into 'dynasties' may rest in these cases on a misinterpretation of older records. Therefore the groupings Fourth, Fifth and Sixth Dynasties are used in this list simply for convenience. Future research and excavation may provide more secure grounds for dividing the Old Kingdom into separate phases.

SNEFERU

The reign of Sneferu witnessed the appearance of the true pyramid, the final development of classic proportions in Egyptian art, and the cartouche, a signal that Pharaonic civilisation had now taken shape. The energy of the reign can be seen in the volume of stone expended on the royal tombs, which surpasses the quantity needed for the Great Pyramid of Khufu. The royal cult centres of Sneferu include the pyramid at Meidum and two more at Dahshur. The king was probably buried at the north Dahshur pyramid. Middle Kingdom tales portray Sneferu as a good, even merry, king.

KHUFU

Builder of the Great Pyramid at Giza, the purest geometric form in human architecture and only surviving Wonder of the World after the classical list. Although it cost less effort than the three pyramids of Sneferu, the sheer size of this one monument earned Khufu a reputation for tyrannical cruelty in later generations. Nothing from the burial of the king survives, but the queen mother, Hetepheres, was robbed soon after her death and her remaining tomb goods reburied, to be rediscovered in 1925 (now in the Egyptian Museum, Cairo).

DJEDEFRA

Eldest son of Khufu and first king to call himself 'son of Ra', though not yet as a fixed title. His pyramid at Abu Roash north of Giza remained unfinished at his death.

KHAFRA

Second son of Khufu and builder of the Second Pyramid at Giza. Though slightly less tall and geometrically less perfect than the Great Pyramid, the Second Pyramid stands on slightly higher ground and retains its top course of fine limestone, lending it a dominant position over the site. The Pyramid Temple and Valley Temple survive, and magnificent statues of the king, of a stone from Nubia known as Toshka diorite, were found in the Valley Temple. The Valley Temple was built south of its proper place on the axis of the Khafra pyramid complex because an outcrop of rock stood in its way. The outcrop was sculpted into a massive lion with the head of Khafra, earliest and largest Egyptian sphinx, called in Arabic 'Father of Dread'.

MENKAURA

Builder of the Third Pyramid at Giza. The pyramid is much smaller than the first two at Giza, but it was covered in a casing of granite and decorated within, both features implying high costs in skilled labour. Statues from the pyramid temples for the royal cult came to be used to provide stone for model vessels for private burials later in the Old Kingdom, but several fine triads of king Menkaura survived.

SHEPSESKAF

This king built not at Giza but south of Saqqara, and chose for his tomb not a pyramid but a cuboid like a sarcophagus, reminiscent of princely tombs at Saqqara in the First Dynasty. His relation to the kings before and after him is not known, but he left a decree exempting the temple of his predecessor Menkaura from various state dues.

Fifth Dynasty, c.2494–2345 BC
The kings who reigned between Shepseskaf and Teti do not form any clear separate group. In a Middle Kingdom tale Userkaf, Sahura and Neferirkara were triplets opening a new royal line, and Teti of the Sixth Dynasty may also have started a new royal family, but the kings between may not all have belonged together. The first kings of this 'dynasty' built at Abusir and set up royal sun-temples as well as pyramids. The sun-temple centred on an open court with a squat colossal obelisk, which represented the sacred benben stone at the solar temple in Heliopolis. Fragments of the exquisite decoration from the royal sun-temples and pyramid complexes are preserved in several museums today, but a number were destroyed in the last war. The last two kings of the 'dynasty' stand out. Isesi ended the practice of building royal sun-temples, and Unas began the custom of inscribing the chambers within the pyramid with funerary texts, and most ancient religious literature

surviving from Egypt. Neferirkara is the first king for whom a second cartouche name is known, Kakai, presumably his birth name. Henceforth both names in cartouches are given wherever known.

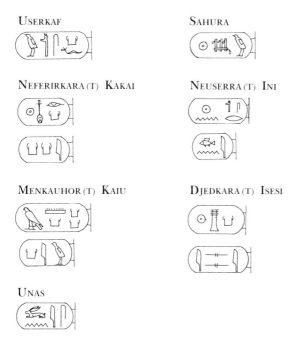

USERKAF

SAHURA

NEFERIRKARA (T) KAKAI

NEUSERRA (T) INI

MENKAUHOR (T) KAIU

DJEDKARA (T) ISESI

UNAS

Sixth Dynasty, c.2345–2181 BC

Possibly singled out by Manetho as members of one family. Pepy I set up life-size copper statues of himself and his infant son at Hieraconpolis. The kinglists credit Pepy II with a reign of 94 years, but this may be a mistake for 64 years, since 60 and 90 can be confused in the cursive hieratic script. His long reign witnessed the evaporation of royal authority at home, and a build-up in foreign settlements on the borders of Egypt, in Nubia to the south and into Sinai to the east.

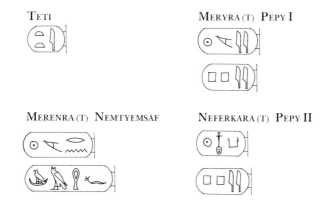

TETI

MERYRA (T) PEPY I

MERENRA (T) NEMTYEMSAF

NEFERKARA (T) PEPY II

Seventh Dynasty

Probably not a group of kings at all, but a device of the ancient historians for marking the collapse of central authority at the end of the Old Kingdom.

Eighth Dynasty, c.2181–2130 BC

Kings ruling, or claiming to rule, Egypt from Memphis, in succession to Pepy II. A royal exemption decree of king Wadjkara and a small pyramid of king Qakara Iby demonstrate how these kings copied Old Kingdom custom but on a sorely reduced scale. No full titulary and only one Horus name (Demedjibtawy, Horus name of Wadjkara on his decreee) can be cited for this period of central weakness.

Ninth and Tenth Dynasties, c.2130–2040 BC

Rulers from Heracleopolis who succeeded the Memphite kings of the Old Kingdom. Their tombs have never been found, and little is known of them. Even a division into two dynasties remains doubtful. Possibly a first group, as the Ninth Dynasty, ruled all Egypt, before a second, the Tenth Dynasty, was confined to the north while Theban princes controlled Upper Egypt. Only one full titulary is known, that of Meryibra Khety, indicating the survival and development of kingship traditions; it includes the earliest known use of the phrase 'son of Ra' as a title set before the cartouche holding the birth name. A literary text of the early Middle Kingdom purports to contain the advice left by a Heracleopolitan king to his successor, Merykara. It comments both on ideal kingship and on specific historical events such as the strengthening of the Eastern Delta border zone and the sacking of the Abydos necropolis during the war with Thebes.

MERYIBRA (T) KHETY   MERYKARA

Eleventh Dynasty, c.2130–1991 BC

(a) Kings ruling only Upper Egypt, from Thebes where they were buried in rock-cut tombs fronted by columned courtyards.

SEHERTAWY INTEF   WAHANKH INTEF

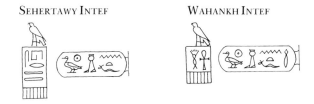

Nakhtnebtepnefer Intef

(b) Kings ruling all Egypt, with full titulary, unlike those of the first group who held only Horus name and birth name.

Nebhepetra (t) Mentuhotep

After a period of fighting against Heracleopolis this king achieved the reunification of Egypt, either by final military victory or through some unrecorded political settlement. His terraced cult temple over his tomb at Deir el-Bahri, Thebes, inspired the terrace temple of Hatshepsut six hundred years later.

Sankhkara (t) Mentuhotep

Like his predecessor, this king ruled all Egypt but built apparently only in Upper Egypt. His additions to local temples include some of the most intricate Egyptian reliefs.

Nebtawyra (t) Mentuhotep

Known only from minor objects and the records of a quarrying expedition which he sent to the Eastern Desert under his vizier Amenemhat. These speak of a miracle of rain, and of another in which a gazelle offered itself for sacrifice. On circumstantial grounds the vizier is often identified today with the following king, Amenemhat I.

Twelfth Dynasty, c.1991–1786 BC

Eight rulers who governed Egypt from a new Residence, Itj-tawy ('Seizer-of-the-Two-Lands'), to the south of Memphis. On the ground secured by the Eleventh Dynasty this family achieved a new peak of prosperity which produced the finest jewellery and the first recorded literary flowering of Egypt. Egypt now dominated her neighbours, Nubia to the south by direct conquest and the removal of settled life, and Palestine to the north-east by diplomacy and intermittent military strikes. In this the height of the Middle Kingdom the fivefold titulary reached its classic form.

SEHETEPIBRA (T) AMENEMHAT I

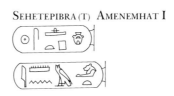

Founded the new Residence, Itj-tawy. A literary masterpiece called 'The Instruction of Amenemhat I' purports to contain the words spoken by the king after his death to his son and successor, Senusret I, in a dream. Here Amenemhat I describes in vivid terms an attempt on his life, at a time when he had not yet designated his son as heir. The episode, if historically accurate, would account for the decision of the king to set his son beside him on the throne as coregent in year 20. The system of coregency ensured smooth succession for the two hundred years of rule by the Twelfth Dynasty. Amenemhat was buried in his pyramid at Lisht.

KHEPERKARA (T) SENUSRET I

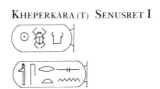

According to another literary jewel, 'The Tale of Sinuhe', this king heard of the news of his father's death while he was on a military campaign in the Western Desert, and had to rush to Itj-tawy. The hero of the tale, Sinuhe misunderstood the king's haste and fled to Palestine where he survived great adventures before returning to Egypt under royal pardon. A further literary manuscript, a leather roll now in Berlin, may record directly a text of the king on the walls of the sun-temple in Heliopolis, relating the decision of the king to build a new monument there. Senusret I completed his father's campaign to subdue Lower Nubia, with the help of fortresses set at strategic points along the river. The king was buried at Lisht.

NUBKAURA (T) AMENEMHAT II

This ruler sent an expedition to the Red Sea to procure incense from the exotic land of Punt. His pyramid complex is at Dahshur, where jewellery of his daughters, princesses Khnumet and Ita the Elder, was discovered in 1895. A block from a temple wall erected by Amenemhat II (perhaps at Heliopolis, although the block was found at Memphis) records the bounty of military and trading expeditions to Western Asia and Punt.

KHAKHEPERRA (T) SENUSRET II

Built a pyramid at Lahun, where jewellery of his daughter, princess Sithathoriunet, was discovered in 1914. An original uraeus from a crown of the king was discovered in his pyramid. Close to his pyramid, Senusret II founded a new town, until recently the only Middle Kingdom town to have survived and been excavated.

KHAKAURA (T) SENUSRET III

New Kingdom stela for the cult of Senusret III and a queen Meresger (named Mereret in Middle Kingdom sources). Height 29 cm. EA 846.

Built a pyramid at Dahshur, where jewellery of his sister, princess Sithathor, and of his queen, Mereret, was discovered in 1895. The king extended the southern border in Nubia and the series of imposing fortresses there. His reign also saw sweeping changes in the hierarchies of government and in the material culture of Egypt, inaugurating the 'late Middle

Kingdom'. This king and his successor have left a unique type of royal portrait in which the king is shown worn by the burden of rule.

NIMAATRA (T) AMENEMHAT III

Was responsible for the pyramid complex at Dahshur and a second at Hawara, thought to be the Labyrinth that astounded Herodotus more than the Great Pyramid for scale and elaborate decoration. The king dispatched virtually yearly a team to work the turquoise veins of Sinai.

MAAKHERURA (T) AMENEMHAT IV

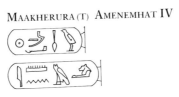

Last king of the Twelfth Dynasty. His burial has not been located.

SOBEKKARA (T) SOBEKNEFERU

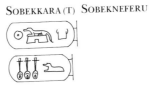

A queen who became the last ruler of the Twelfth Dynasty, with full fivefold titulary. It is assumed that she became queen because Amenemhat IV died without a male heir. Her tomb has never been found.

Thirteenth Dynasty, c.1786–1674 BC

Kings ruling from Itj-tawy, with authority over all Egypt at least until king Ay. No single royal family followed the Twelfth Dynasty; instead, the kings came from varied backgrounds and each reigned for on average only about five years. Although these short reigns excluded major expoits in building or foreign ventures, Egypt saw little change in government and way of life until about the reign of king Ay. Four small Thirteenth Dynasty pyramids survive at Saqqara, but after king Ay's reign the kings at Itj-tawy seem to have lost control of the Eastern Delta and their activity was gradually reduced to the Theban area.

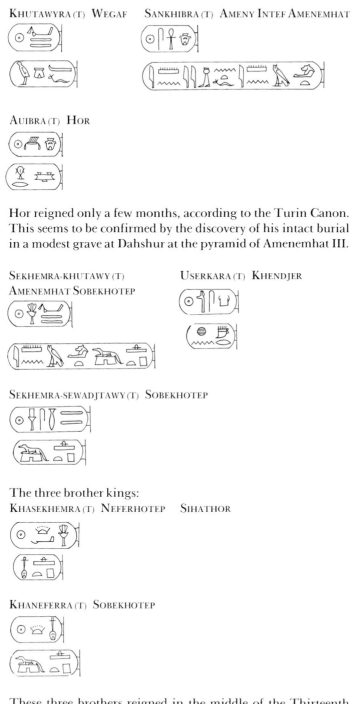

KHUTAWYRA (T) WEGAF

SANKHIBRA (T) AMENY INTEF AMENEMHAT

AUIBRA (T) HOR

Hor reigned only a few months, according to the Turin Canon. This seems to be confirmed by the discovery of his intact burial in a modest grave at Dahshur at the pyramid of Amenemhat III.

SEKHEMRA-KHUTAWY (T)
AMENEMHAT SOBEKHOTEP

USERKARA (T) KHENDJER

SEKHEMRA-SEWADJTAWY (T) SOBEKHOTEP

The three brother kings:
KHASEKHEMRA (T) NEFERHOTEP   SIHATHOR

KHANEFERRA (T) SOBEKHOTEP

These three brothers reigned in the middle of the Thirteenth Dynasty, an isolated moment of strong rule and continuity on the throne. Neferhotep is shown on a relief at Byblos receiving the adulation of the local town prince. He and Sobekhotep launched the only known Thirteenth Dynasty expeditions for valuable stone in the Eastern Desert. The third brother, Sihathor, appears on several monuments as a prince, but attestations of him as a king Menwadjra (T) have been disputed.

MERNEFERRA (T) AY

The last Thirteenth Dynasty king whose monuments survive in both Upper and Lower Egypt. The Eastern Delta probably seceded soon after his death.

SEKHEMRA-SANKHTAWY (T) IYKHERNOFRET NEFERHOTEP

Fourteenth Dynasty, *c.*1700–1674 BC

These kings ruled the Eastern Delta during the late Thirteenth Dynasty. Only two are known from contemporary monuments.

AASEHRA (T) NEHESY

Fifteenth Dynasty, *c.*1674–1567 BC

'Desert kings', in Egyptian *Hyksos*, ruling northern Egypt after the Thirteenth and Fourteenth Dynasties. Only Khyan and Apepi left large monuments, but Yannas, the son of Khyan, is named on a block recently discovered at Tell ed-Daba in the Eastern Delta. The kinglists cite six Hyksos who ruled from Avaris, probably Tell ed-Daba. Apepi and Khyan held Horus names and cartouches but not a full titulary of five royal names. Apepi fought with the successors of the Thirteenth Dynasty, the Seventeenth Dynasty at Thebes, who emerged victorious. In the course of his long reign he changed his throne name twice.

SEUSERENRA(T) KHYAN AAUSERRA(T) APEPI

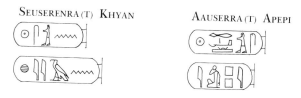

Sixteenth Dynasty, c.1674–1567 BC

Minor rulers, usually identified as the kings known only from scarabs in Egypt and Palestine. They presumably lay under the shadow of Avaris.

ANATHER YAKOBAAM

Seventeenth Dynasty, c.1674–1567 BC

Kings in succession to the Thirteenth Dynasty, but confined to Upper Egypt and buried at Dra Abu el-Nega at Thebes. Several of their bodies and burial goods were collected and reburied at the end of the New Kingdom, to be rediscovered in the last century. The early kings took full titularies and their monuments can scarcely be distinguished from those of the late Thirteenth Dynasty. The last two kings of the dynasty undertook the wars against the Hyksos. According to a New Kingdom story, the first dispute was in the reign of Seqenenra Taa. His body survives, and his skull bears the imprint of an axe-type used under the Hyksos. The next king, Kamose, laid siege to the Hyksos capital, Avaris, but died before a successful outcome. His successor achieved final victory, ushering in a new age.

NUBKHEPERRA(T) INTEF SEKHEMRA-WADJKHAU(T) SOBEKEMSAF
(probably in this dynasty)

SEQENENRA(T) TAA(qen) WADJKHEPERRA(T) KAMOSE

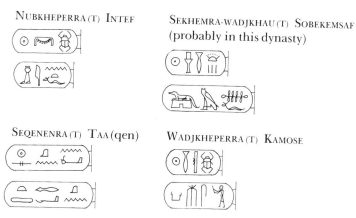

Eighteenth Dynasty, c.1567–1320 BC

The first king of this dynasty, Ahmose I, was a son of Seqenenra Taa and completed the victory of Thebes over Avaris. The ensuing kings brought Egyptian armies deep into Syria-Palestine and Nubia, creating an age of spectacular luxury, the New Kingdom. The dynasty is marked by the exceptional reigns of Hatshepsut, the queen who claimed kingship, and Akhenaten, the king who transformed Egyptian religion. Both reigns were condemned by posterity and the legitimacy of both rulers denied. The kings from Amenhotep I onwards were buried in the Valley of the Kings at Thebes, except for Akhenaten who sited his tomb at his Residence, Amarna. Most of the royal bodies were collected at the end of the New Kingdom to be reburied in safer caches; they were rediscovered in the late nineteenth century and are now in the Egyptian Museum, Cairo. The tomb of Tutankhamun escaped detection and was discovered virtually intact in 1922 by Howard Carter.

NEBPEHTYRA (T) AHMOSE I   DJESERKARA (T) AMENHOTEP I

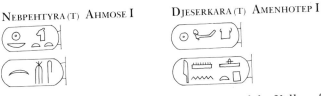

Amenhotep I was founder and patron deity of the Valley of the Kings.

AAKHEPERKARA (T) THUTMOSE I

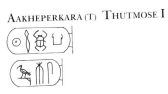

This king did not belong to the family of Ahmose and Amenhotep I. His armies reached the distant bounds of Syria and Upper Nubia. In his reign the Amun temple at Karnak underwent extensive restoration.

AAKHEPERENRA (T) THUTMOSE II

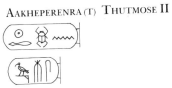

This son of Thutmose I reigned only briefly and was eclipsed by his half-sister, Hatshepsut.

M<small>AATKARA</small> (<small>T</small>) H<small>ATSHEPSUT</small> (-amun)

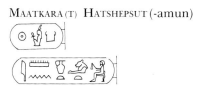

Against the norms of Egyptian kingship, this queen claimed to be king and undertook royal initiatives such as despatching expeditions abroad and building a temple for her own cult. Her temple, at Deir el-Bahri, remains one of the most original and stirring monuments in Egypt, a set of terraces against the backdrop of the Theban mountain. Equally beautiful are her inscribed monolithic obelisks of Aswan granite, set up at the Amun temple in Karnak. The drama of their quarrying, transport and erection is depicted in the walls of her temple at Deir el-Bahri. Although she reigned alongside her young nephew Thutmose III, he erased her claims to kingship after her death, more probably out of orthodox belief than out of malice.

M<small>ENKHEPERRA</small> (<small>T</small>) T<small>HUTMOSE</small> III

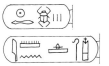

Named the Napoleon of Egypt for his military exploits, but also from an erroneous measurement of the height of his mummy. Before and after the death of his step-mother and coregent, Hatshepsut, he conducted incessant campaigns to secure the northern and southern borders of Egypt and Upper Nubia. His reign marks a turning point in the Egyptian way of life, both for the increase in foreign contacts and influence and for the wealth from control of northern tradelines and Nubian goldmines. His inscriptions at Karnak record the lavish donations he made to the Amun temple there.

A<small>AKHEPERURA</small> (<small>T</small>) A<small>MENHOTEP</small> (heqa-iunu) II

Continued his father's military campaigns, emphasising his own physical prowess as a charioteer and archer in poetic texts on his monuments.

MENKHEPERURA (T) THUTMOSE IV

On a stela set between the paws of the Giza Sphinx the king describes how as a prince he fell asleep during a day of hunting in the desert. In his sleep he dreamed that the Sphinx, identified in the New Kingdom as the sun-god rather than as king Khafra of the Fourth Dynasty, promised him the throne in return for clearing the sand that engulfed it. The king complied and recorded the tale on the stela, still in place.

NEBMAATRA (T) AMENHOTEP (heqa-waset) III

Ruled Egypt at the height of her prosperity and luxury: letters from foreign kings to Amenhotep III claim that gold was as plentiful as dust in Egypt. With this wealth Amenhotep III launched a spectacular programme of building temples, particularly in Thebes. He not only enlarged the Amun temple at Karnak, but created entire new temples at Luxor for Amun, at South Karnak for the goddess Mut, and on the West Bank for his own cult. On the West Bank he also constructed a pleasure palace with a great harbour and magnificent wall-paintings. The colossal statues in front of his cult temple, the Colossi of Memnon, attracted Greek and Roman tourists, because a fissure in one of them caused it to 'sing' at daybreak. Today they are all that remains of the once splendid cult temple. At the temple of Mut Amenhotep III installed hundreds of statues of Mut in the form of a lioness-headed goddess, the raging Sekhmet. These are today scattered on the site and in museums throughout the world.

NEFERKHEPERURA-WAENRA (T) AKHENATEN

Akhenaten is famous for his short-lived transformation of Egyptian art and religion. He reduced royal worship to a cult of the physical sun disc Aton and built for him a temple behind the Amun temple at Karnak (only blocks of this survive today). His birth name, Amenhotep, was changed to Akhenaten, meaning 'Beneficial to the Aton', to proclaim his devotion. In the sixth year of his reign he created a new city for the god, called Akhetaten ('Horizon of the Aton') at Amarna in Middle Egypt. Throughout Egypt the name of Amun was erased, and royal agents also destroyed images of Hapy, the Inundation deity Mut, and any mention of 'the gods' in texts. In private homes only the royal family were worshipped. Osiris, god of the dead, disappeared from official art, which developed new proportions and portrayed the king as a fertility god, replacing Hapy, with elongated and feminine features. At Amarna an entire sculptor's studio was found, with royal portrait heads, including the famous head of queen Nefertiti. The bodies of the royal family were never found, except those of Tutankhamun and a prince about twenty years old, buried in a royal coffin in a minor grave in the Valley of the Kings.

ANKHKHEPERURA (T) SMENKHKARA (djeser-kheperu)

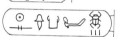

The identity of this ruler is currently disputed. Some scholars regard Smenkhkara as a throne name taken by queen Nefertiti, and claim that she ruled alongside and after Akhenaten. Others consider Smenkhkara to be a contemporary of Tutankhamun, and identify him with the prince buried in the royal coffin in the Valley of the Kings.

NEBKHEPERURA (T) TUTANKHAMUN (heqa-iunu-shema)

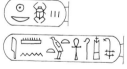

Tutankhamun was born Tutankhaton ('living image of the Aton') but changed the Aton in his name to Amun when he came to the throne as a boy. Under his rule the court abandoned Amarna, and Egypt returned to the old religion and art; the name of Amun was restored, those of Akhenaten destroyed. The virtually intact tomb of the boy king was found in 1922.

KHEPERKHEPERURA-IRMAAT (T) AY (it-netjer)

An elderly courtier who buried Tutankhamun and claimed the throne.

DJESERKHEPERURA-SETEPENRA (T) HOREMHEB (meryamun)

The general of Tutankhamun, whose private tomb at Saqqara was seen by Lepsius in the 1840s and rediscovered in 1975. Upon the death of Ay he became king, constructed a royal tomb for himself in the Valley of the Kings, and took over the restoration of monuments ruined by Akhenaten by replacing the names of Ay and Tutankhamun with his own.

Nineteenth Dynasty, c.1320–1200 BC

MENPEHTYRA (T) RAMSES I

An elderly military officer selected as successor by Horemheb, perhaps conscious of Ramses' talented son, Sety.

MENMAATRA (T) SETY (meryenptah) I

In this reign the restoration programme initiated by Tutankhamun reached its climax, with royal cult temples at Abydos and the Theban West Bank, and work on a columned hall of unprecedented size at Karnak, the Hypostyle Hall completed by Ramses II. The king led armies abroad to secure the boundaries of Egypt, echoing the achievements of kings of the Eighteenth Dynasty before Akhenaten. The sculpted relief of this reign attained a degree of refinement rarely excelled, particularly in the colourful scenes of the Abydos temple and the royal tomb in the Valley of the Kings. The tomb, the deepest and longest in the Valley, established an entirely new type of layout, an extended tunnel decorated with elaborate representations of the journey of the sun, incorporating the king, through the night sky and the mysteries of solar rebirth.

Usermaatra-setepenra (t) Ramses (meryamun) II

In his reign of sixty-four years, Ramses II transformed the face of Egypt by the sheer quantity of his monuments. Scarcely a town in Egypt or Nubia escaped his attention, and today his statues and temples ensure that he remains the best-known builder Pharaoh. In Greek his throne name is read Ozymandias, whose statue (probably the ruined thousand-ton colossus at the Theban royal cult temple, the Ramesseum) served Shelley as the model for the vain arrogance of the powerful in his poem of the same name. The king founded a new royal Residence called Piramses ('House of Ramses') in the Eastern Delta, near the site of the old city of the Hyksos, Avaris. Wars against Hittite kings ended in a truce, the oldest surviving international treaty; one battle at Kadesh brought the king close to disaster, avoided only by a show of classic royal bravura and a Hittite miscalculation. The king had this battle immortalised in a long epic and a shorter poem recorded on the main entrance pylon at Luxor temple, and on the walls of temples to the royal cult at Western Thebes, Abydos and in Nubia at Abu Simbel. This last is the greatest of a series of New Kingdom rock temples. When the new Aswan dam threatened to engulf the monuments of Nubia in a reservoir, the twin temples of the king and his queen, Nefertari, at Abu Simbel were among the sites rescued through modern technology, cut block by block out of the mountainside and rebuilt on higher, safer, ground. Queen Nefertari was buried in the most beautiful Theban tomb, in the Valley of the Queens, closed in recent years because of the instability of the painted plaster. A few items of jewellery of Ramses II were discovered in the Saqqara tomb of his son Khaemwaset, often called the first Egyptologist for his pious works restoring already ancient monuments. The king's own tomb has been badly damaged by flooding.

BAENRA-MERYNETJERU (T) MERENPTAH (hetep-her-maat)

Fragment of the alabaster sarcophagus of Merenptah, identified by his cartouches (top left). Height 30.5 cm. EA 49739.

Often said to be the king of the Hebrew Exodus, but on no scientific grounds. The king fought defensive campaigns against northern enemies, and a victory stela of his reign includes the sole mention of Israel in Egyptian texts.

USERKHEPERURA-SETEPENRA (T) SETY (merenptah) II

The tomb reliefs and surviving statues of this king indicate the renewal, for a brief time, of fine artistic accomplishment during his reign.

MENMIRA-SETEPENRA (T) AMENMESSE (heqa-waset)

AKHENRA-SETEPENRA (T) SIPTAH (merenptah)

SITRA-MERYAMUN (T) TAUSRET (setepetenmut)

Golden earring with the birth
name of Queen Tausret. Thebes.
Diameter 2.5 cm. EA 54459.

The course of events after the death of Sety II is unclear but
turns on the role of queen Tausret, who claimed kingship
alongside or after king Siptah. She appears to have been the
wife of king Sety II, under whom a king Amenmesse usurped
power at least in Upper Egypt. Twentieth Dynasty texts claim
that they restored order after chaos caused by an alien lord
called Bay, probably the foreign First Minister of queen
Tausret.

Twentieth Dynasty, c.1200–1085 BC

USERKHAURA-SETEPENRA (T)
SETNAKHT (mereramunra)

USERMAATRA-MERYAMUN (T)
RAMSES (heqa-iunu) III

The last great temple builder of the New Kingdom, with a
wayshrine for Amun at Karnak and a largely intact royal cult
temple at Medinet Habu on the Theban West Bank. The walls
of the latter record his battles against northern foes, the so-called
Sea Peoples.

HEQAMAATRA (T) RAMSES IV

NEBMAATRA-MERYAMUN (T)
RAMSES (amunherkhepshef-
netjerheqaiunu) VI

NEFERKARA-SETEPENRA (T)
RAMSES (khaemwaset-
mereramun) IX

MENMAATRA-SETEPENPTAH (T)
RAMSES (khaemwaset-mereramun-
netjerheqaiunu) XI

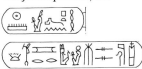

This king began, but never completed, the last royal tomb to be built in the Valley of the Kings. In year 19 of his reign rebellion by the Viceroy of Kush, Panehesy, brought about a formal rearrangement of the state, the 'repeating of births' or 'Renaissance'. Under the Renaissance Ramses XI continued to reign from Piramses, but power was held by one Nesbanebdjed (Smendes) in the north and the general Herihor at Thebes. Herihor became High Priest of Amun and claimed royal status.

Theban ruler (with cartouches) at the end of the Twentieth Dynasty:

HEMNETJERTEPYENAMUN (T, meaning 'High Priest of Amun')
HERIHOR (siamun)

Twenty-First Dynasty, c.1085–945 BC

Kings ruling from Tanis, a new city north of Piramses. They allowed the Theban rulers to retain control over Upper Egyptian affairs, apparently on amicable terms. Only two Theban rulers, general Pinudjem and High Priest Menkheperra, claimed kingship as Herihor had; all the other Theban rulers held the title High Priest of Amun. They were buried with certain of the royal mummies from the Valley of the Kings in a cache at Deir el-Bahri. The northern kings were buried in the precincts of the Amun temple at Tanis. In 1939 part of the royal necropolis at Tanis was discovered, including the burials of king Pasebakhaenniut (Psusennes) I and king Amenemopet. Their bodies and treasure now rest in the Egyptian Museum, Cairo.

HEDJKHEPERRA-SETEPENRA (T)   NESBANEBDJED (meryamun)
(SMENDES)

AAKHEPERRA-SETEPENAMUN (T) PASEBAKHAENNIUT (meryamun)
(PSUSENNES) I

This king seems to have been responsible for moving a city of colossal statuary and granite blocks from Piramses to Tanis, where most still lie toppled. In his intact burial was found the sarcophagus of Merenptah, which can only have reached Tanis from Thebes with local cooperation. One of his daughters, Istemkheb, married the Theban High Priest Menkheperra.

USERMAATRA-MERYAMUN-
SETEPENAMUN (T)
AMENEMOPET

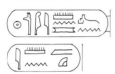

NETJERKHEPERRA-SETEPENAMUN (T)
SIAMON

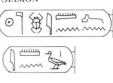

TITKHEPERURA-SETEPENRA (T) PASEBAKHAENNIUT (meryamun)
(PSUSENNES) II

Theban rulers claiming royal status (with cartouches):

KHAKHEPERRA-SETEPENAMUN (T)
PINUDJEM (meryamun) (I)

HEMNETJERTEPYENAMUN
(T, meaning 'High Priest of Amun')
MENKHEPERRA

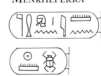

Twenty-Second Dynasty, c.945–715 BC

Kings ruling from Tanis, coming from a northwestern tribe, the Meshwesh. Initially they restored royal authority over all Egypt, and even launched military campaigns into Palestine. Thebes retained a certain autonomy, with princes of the royal house appointed as High Priests of Amun. From the reign of Sheshonq III the Tanite kings lost their authority and had to rule alongside a growing number of rival kings throughout Egypt, the Twenty-Third Dynasty. Kings of the Twenty-Second Dynasty were buried in the Twenty-First Dynasty royal necropolis at Tanis, where the burials of Osorkon II, Sheshonq II and Sheshonq III were discovered in 1939. The popularity of the cat, sacred at Bubastis, may be traced to this period.

HEDJKHEPERRA-SETEPENRA (T) SHESHONQ (meryamun) I

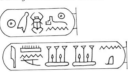

Born into a Meshwesh family at Bubastis, Sheshonq I was a general under Pasebakhaenniut (Psusennes) II before he became king. He imposed his rule over Thebes by appointing his son, Iuput, as High Priest of Amun. Abroad, he led Egyptian troops into Palestine for the first time since the New Kingdom, and returned with 'tribute' from various cities, including Jerusalem. At Karnak he cut out a great gateway with a relief recording his Asiatic campaign.

SEKHEMKHEPERRA (T) OSORKON I

HEQAKHEPERRA-SETEPENRA (T)
SHESHONQ (meryamun) II

USERMAATRA-SETEPENAMUN (T) OSORKON (meryamun) II

This king constructed a great temple hall at Bubastis to commemorate his *sed* or jubilee festival. His burial was discovered at Tanis in 1939.

HEDJKHEPERRA-SETEPENRA (T)
TAKELOT (meryamun) II

USERMAATRA-SETEPENRA (T)
SHESHONQ (meryamun) III

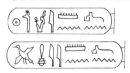

USERMAATRA-SETEPENAMUN (T)   PAMIY (setepenamun)

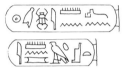

Princes who claimed kingship in Thebes as High Priests of Amun:

HEDJKHEPERRA-SETEPENAMUN (T)   HORSIESE (meryamun)

Other High Priests of Amun claimed cartouches, probably as Crown Princes, whereas Horsiese never became king of all Egypt. He 'reigned' under the powerful northern king Osorkon II, and was buried at Medinet Habu.

Twenty-Third Dynasty, c.818–715 BC

In the reign of Sheshonq III of Tanis, Thebes began to recognise a rival king, Padibastet (Petubastis). Thereafter central authority collapsed, with separate kings taking throne names and cartouches in various towns. Only two of these 'Twenty-Third Dynasty' kings held full titularies with the five royal names, Osorkon (III) and Takelot (III), perhaps both at Thebes. In the morasse of names and epithets it is often difficult to determine the order and identity, and so the numbering, of these kings.

USERMAATRA-SETEPENAMUN (T)
PADIBASTET (meryamun) (I)
At Thebes.

USERMAATRA (T)
IUPUT (meryamun-sibastet) (II)
At Leontopolis.

NIMLOT
At Hermopolis.

NEFERKARA (T) PEFTJAUABASTET
At Heracleopolis.

Twenty-Fourth Dynasty, c.727–715 BC

During the chaos of the late Twenty-Second Dynasty in the eighth century BC, one of the rival groups of kings was the ruling family of Sais in the Western Delta. Although they were defeated by the Twenty-Fifth Dynasty, they had begun to establish a solid power base, recovered in the seventh century BC by the Twenty-Sixth Dynasty of Sais.

SHEPSESRA (T) TEFNAKHT

WAHKARA (T) BAKENRENEF
(BOCCHORIS)

Twenty-Fifth Dynasty, c.747–656 BC

Kings from Kush, ancient kingdom to the south of Nubia. They resided at Napata, and were buried in pyramids at Kurru, except Taharqa who was buried in a pyramid at Nuri. In the second half of the eighth century BC these southern kings established control over Egypt in a series of invasions. The

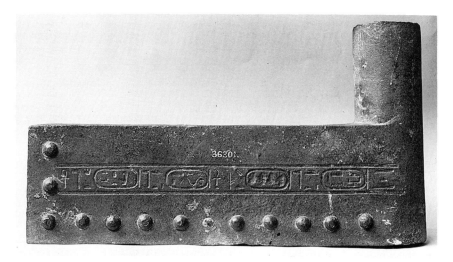

Bronze fitting with the cartouches of high priestesses of Amun and (erased) Pi(ankh)i. Height 20.4 cm. EA 36301.

best attested intervention is that of Pi(ankh)i, recorded on a stela that gives every detail of the royal conquest. It is still debated whether the *ankh* in his name belongs to the name Piankhi, or whether it expresses the wish 'May he live!' with a simple name, Piy. Shabako is thought to have achieved the final defeat of the various kings of the Twenty-Second to Twenty-Fourth Dynasties, in *c*.715 BC, and his reign restored stability in Egypt, revitalising art and monumental activity. He had the Memphite myth of creation carved on a slab of basalt, allegedly after finding the text worm-eaten in the temple library. The Kushite kings brought a return to classic forms in the royal names, and displayed particular reverence to the cult of Amun in an echo of the New Kingdom. Under Taharqo an imposing portico was added to the temple entrance at Karnak, emblematic of the energy of the period. Kushite rule over Egypt ended with the Assyrian invasions, in 671 BC against Taharqo and in 663 BC against Tanutamani. Upper Egypt recognised Tanutamani until 656 BC, but then acknowledged the rule of the Saite Twenty-Sixth Dynasty. In Kush the kings from Tanutamani onwards continued to use Egyptian forms of kingship, including cartouches for their names and burial in pyramids.

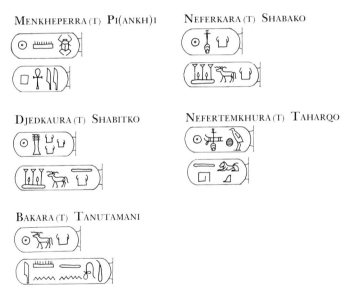

MENKHEPERRA (T) PI(ANKH)I

NEFERKARA (T) SHABAKO

DJEDKAURA (T) SHABITKO

NEFERTEMKHURA (T) TAHARQO

BAKARA (T) TANUTAMANI

Twenty-Sixth Dynasty, *c*.664–525 BC

Kings from Sais. The Assyrians selected Egyptian governors to control Egypt for them and prevent the Kushite kings from returning. After the second Assyrian invasion the Saite ruling family successfully kept the southern kings at bay, and took advantage of Assyrian preoccupations to achieve independence. Psamtek I became king with a full fivefold titulary, and established his authority at Thebes in 656 BC by having his daughter, Nitocret, adopted as successor by the Kushite High Priestess or 'God's Wife' of Amun, with the blessing of the Theban governor Montuemhat. On the foundations laid by the Kushite kings, Egypt enjoyed a new golden age of prosperity and creativity, the Late Period. Psamtek II replied to Kushite aggression with a campaign against Napata, causing the Kushite kings to move their capital south to Meroe. The era was cut short by the Persian invasion in 525 BC in the reign of Psamtek III.

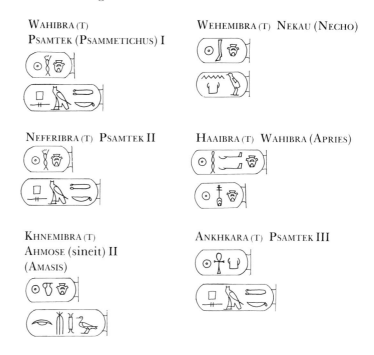

WAHIBRA (T)
PSAMTEK (PSAMMETICHUS) I

WEHEMIBRA (T) NEKAU (NECHO)

NEFERIBRA (T) PSAMTEK II

HAAIBRA (T) WAHIBRA (APRIES)

KHNEMIBRA (T)
AHMOSE (sineit) II
(AMASIS)

ANKHKARA (T) PSAMTEK III

Twenty-Seventh Dynasty or First Persian Period, 525–404 BC

The first Persian kings to rule Egypt, Cambyses and Darius, behaved as Pharaohs, taking Horus name and cartouches and building at temple sites such as the Khargeh Oasis shrine. Xerxes I and Artaxerxes I also had their names written in cartouches, although they took no Egyptian names. Rebellions against Persia led to retribution and more oppressive rule, until the revolt of Amyrtaeus in 404 BC brought independence.

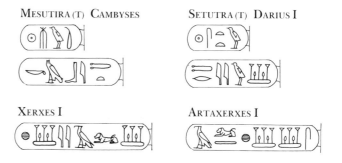

MESUTIRA (T) CAMBYSES

SETUTRA (T) DARIUS I

XERXES I

ARTAXERXES I

Rebel kings against the Persians:

SEHERIBRA (T)   INAROS
PADIBASTET (PEDUBASTIS)   (Not attested in hieroglyphs)

Twenty-Eighth Dynasty, 404–399 BC

This 'dynasty' contains only Amyrtaeus, the Saite prince who rebelled successfully against Persia with the aid of Sparta. He left no monument with a hieroglyphic writing of his name. The Demotic Chronicle, a unique demotic text written in the late third century BC, interprets the fate of rulers of the Twenty-Eighth to Thirtieth Dynasties as proof that piety brings success, impiety disaster. It implies that Amyrtaeus was executed by the prince of Mendes, Nefaarud (Nepherites), and for his name suggests the Egyptian form Amenirdis.

Twenty-Ninth Dynasty, 399–380 BC

Kings from Mendes ruling all Egypt, none of whose tombs have been located. The founder of the dynasty, Nefaarud (Nepherites), built monuments in both the Nile Delta and Valley. His successor, Pashemut (Psammuthis), was replaced by an unrelated prince of Mendes, Hakor, who pursued an active building programme and sealed foreign alliances to keep out the Persians. Hakor held the first full royal titulary since the Twenty-Sixth Dynasty.

BAENRA-MERYNETJERU (T)   MAATIBRA (T) HAKOR
NEFAARUD (NEPHERITES) I

Thirtieth Dynasty, 380–343 BC

At the end of the reign of Hakor, revolts broke out and the last king of Mendes, Nefaarud (Nepherites) II, was dethroned. His place was taken by a general from Sebennytus, Nakhtnebef (Nectanebo I), who seems to have been related to the family of Nefaarud (Nepherites) I. The art of Nakhtnebef's reign took the Twenty-Sixth Dynasty as its model. His son and successor, Djedhor (Tachos or Teos), imposed heavy taxes in his bid to conquer Syria from Persia; these caused a rebellion through which his nephew, Nakhthorheb (Nectanebo II), became king. Nakhthorheb added to temples throughout

Egypt, both in monuments and in generous donations. His reign ended with the second Persian conquest of Egypt in 343 BC.

KHEPERKARA (T)
NAKHTNEBEF (NECTANEBO I)

IRMAATENRA (T)
DJEDHOR (setepeninhur)

SENEDJEMIBRA-SETEPENINHUR (T)
NAKHTHORHEB (meryhathor)
(NECTANEBO II)

Thirty-First Dynasty or Second Persian Period, 343–332 BC
During the reconquest Artaxerxes III gained a reputation for mindless cruelty. It may be more than coincidence that we have not found any hieroglyphic writing of his name. After the murder of the king in 338 BC a certain Khababash established his rule for a couple of years in at least part of Egypt. The last Persian king, Darius III, regained control of Egypt, and had his name written in hieroglyphs. He lost his Empire to Alexander the Great.

DARIUS III

Kings of Macedon in Egypt, 332–305 BC
Alexander the Great took the role of Pharaoh in Egypt and bagan the task of restoring temples damaged in 343 BC at the second Persian conquest. Nevertheless, he retained the Persian system of government under which Egypt formed the Sixth Satrapy of the Empire. At the mouth of the West branch of the Nile Delta Alexander founded a new city, Alexandria. After his death his half-brother, Philip Arrhidaeus, and son, Alexander IV, became joint kings of Macedon. Ptolemy, son of Lagus, the Macedonian satrap in Egypt, took the body of Alexander the Great to be buried in Alexandria; the tomb is now lost. Court intrigue led to the murder of Philip Arrhidaeus in 317 BC and of Alexander IV in 311 BC, although official texts continued to refer to Alexander IV as king until 305 BC, when the satrap Ptolemy proclaimed himself king of Egypt.

MERYAMUN-SETEPENRA (T)
ALEXANDER THE GREAT

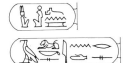

MERYAMUN-SETEPENRA (T)
PHILIP ARRHIDAEUS

HAAIBRA-SETEPENAMUN (T)
ALEXANDER IV

The Ptolemies, 305–30 BC

Macedonian kings ruling all Egypt from Alexandria. The Ptolemies lived a double life, as rulers of the most brilliant Hellenistic court and as Greek-speaking Pharaohs lavishing donations and monuments on the temples of Egypt. In the third century BC this double act brought wealth and stability at home, and extensive dominions abroad. The lighthouse on Pharos, by the harbour of Alexandria, and the famous Library of Ptolemy II brought the city glory in commerce and learning. At the close of the third century BC Ptolemy IV lost control of much of Egypt to rebels in the Nile Valley and Delta. Under his son, the child king Ptolemy V, the Alexandrian troops succeeded in defeating first the Delta rebels and then the independent kings of Upper Egypt. Priests convened at Memphis decreed a divine cult for the boy king, in Egyptian style, after the Delta victory. This decree was to be engraved in three scripts, hieroglyphic, cursive demotic and Greek, and set up in every temple. One version was found at Rosetta in 1799 and led to the decipherment of the hieroglyphs. Although the Ptolemaic forces were able to reconquer all of Egypt by 186 BC, the dynasty never recovered the strength of the third century BC and fell under the rising star of Rome. The last Ptolemaic queen, Cleopatra VII, attempted to forge a new power with the aid of Roman military leaders: she made Caesarion, her son by Julius Caesar, child king, and gained the allegiance of Mark Anthony. Upon his defeat by Octavian she committed suicide and her son was murdered.

MERYAMUN-SETEPENRA (T)
PTOLEMY I

USERKAENRA-MERYAMUN (T)
PTOLEMY II

IWAENNETJERWYSENWY-SEKHEMANKHRA-SETEPAMUN (T)
PTOLEMY (ankhdjet-meryptah) III

IWAENNETJERWYMENKHWY-SETEPPTAH-USERKARA-SEKHEMANKHAMUN (T)
PTOLEMY (ankhdjet-meryese) IV

IWAENNETJERWYMERWYITU-SETEPPTAH-USERKARA-SEKHEMANKHAMUN (T)
PTOLEMY (ankhdjet-meryptah) V

IWAENNETJERWYPER-SETEPENPTAHKHEPRI-IRMAATENAMUNRA (T)
PTOLEMY IV

IWAENPANETJERNEHEM-SETEPPTAH-IRMAAT (T)
PTOLEMY (ankhdjet-meryptah-siese) XII

IWAPANETJERENTYNEHEM-SETEPENPTAH-IRMAATENRA-
SEKHEMANKHAMUN (T)
PTOLEMY XV CAESARION

CLEOPATRA (netjeret-merites)VII

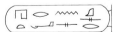

Rebel kings against the Ptolemies, 205–186 BC, no hieroglyphic source:

HORWENNEFER, 205–199 BC   ANKHWENNEFER, 199–86 BC

Roman Emperors, 30 BC-AD 305 (latest secure hieroglyphic royal names)
Egypt became a unique province of the Roman Empire, personal domain of the Emperor. Few Emperors displayed active interest but monuments were still built in the name of the reigning 'Pharaoh'.

AUTOCRATOR (T) KAISAROS (AUGUSTUS)   TIBERIUS

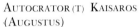

HORSIESE-MERYNETJERUNEBU (T) DOMITIAN (entykhu)

AUTOCRATOR-KAISAROS-NERVO (T) TRAJANUS (entykhu) (TRAJAN)

HADRIANUS-CAESAR (HADRIAN)   DIOCLETIAN

Appendix: **Kushite rulers after the expulsion of Tanutamani from Egypt**
The rulers at Napata continued to take Egyptian titularies. Aspelta was the king contemporary with Psamtek II of Egypt and moved his capital to Meroe, probably after the Egyptian campaign against Napata. The Meroitic kings continued to take Horus names and cartouches, and one of them, Harsiotef, held not only a full fivefold titulary but also an Egyptian birth name. One king at Meroe, Amanislo, had his name carved on lions of Amenhotep III from Soleb, now in the British Museum (EA 1 and 2). The Egyptologist Mariette read the name as Amonasro, and used it for the Ethiopian king in his libretto for Verdi's opera *Aida*. Natakamani, in the first century AD, was one of the last Meroitic kings to write his names in Egyptian hieroglyphs and cartouches. Among his many monuments stands the temple at Naga to the Meroitic lion god Apedemak.

MERKARA (T) ASPELTA

SIMERYAMUN (T) HARSIOTEF

ANKHNEFERIBRA (T) AMANISLO

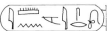

KHEPERKARA (T) NATAKAMANI

Faience *shabti* of Aspelta, king of Kush. Nuri.
Height 25.5 cm. EA 55511.

Bibliography

Beckerath, Jürgen von, *Handbuch der ägyptischen Königsnamen*, Münchner Ägyptologischen Studien 20, Munich and Berlin, 1984

Beckerath, Jürgen von, 'Königsnamen', in Wolfgang Helck and Wolfhart Westendorf (eds), *Lexikon der Ägyptologie*, vol. III, Wiesbaden, 1980, 540–56

Davies, W.V., *Egyptian Hieroglyphs*, London, 1987

Gauthier, Henri, *Le Livre des Rois d'Egypte*, Mémoires publiés par les membres de l'Institut Français d'Archéologie Orientale au Caire nos. 17–21, 5 vols, Cairo, 1907–17

Kaplony, Peter, 'Königsring', in Wolfgang Helck and Wolfhart Westendorf (eds), *Lexikon der Ägyptologie*, vol. III, Wiesbaden, 1980, 610–26

Kaplony, Peter, 'Königstitulatur', in Wolfgang Helck and Wolfhart Westendorf (eds), *Lexikon der Ägyptologie*, vol. III, Wiesbaden, 1980, 641–59

Lichtheim, Miriam, *Ancient Egyptian Literature*, 3 vols, Berkeley, 1975–80. A selection that includes many of the most important literary texts concerning kingship

Wildung, Dieter, *Die Rolle ägyptischer Könige im Bewusstsein ihrer Nachwelt*, Münchner Ägyptologischen Studien 17, Munich and Berlin, 1969

Index of rulers

cited in Chapters 1-4

References in italic type are to illustrations.

Adjib 22,23
Aha 20,*20*,21,22
Ahmose I 31
Akhenaten 32,*32*,33
Alexander the Great (III of Macedon) 40
Alexander IV of Macedon 40
Amenemhat I 19,29
Amenemhat III 15,*15*
Amyrtaeus 39
Antoninus Pius 43
Artaxerxes III 40
Augustus 42
Ay 32,33

Berenice (II) 42

Cambyses 39
Cleopatra (VII) 42

Darius I 39
Den 22,*22*,23
Diocletian 43
Djedefra 25
Djer 22,23
Djet 22,23
Djoser 25
Domitian 43

Hatshepsut 14,15,16,*16*,32,42
Horemheb 32,33,*33*,34

Inarus 39
Intef (Seventeenth Dynasty) *31*

Ka 21,*21*
Kakai *see* Neferirkara Kakai
Khaankhra Sobekhotep *31*
Khasekhemwy 24
Khafra 25,29
Khufu 16,25
Khyan *31*

Menkaura 25,*26*
Merenptah 39
Meryibra Khety 27

Nakhtnebef 39,*40*
Narmer 21,22
Nebhepetra Mentuhotep 27
Nebra 24

Nefaarud 39
Neferirkara Kakai 17,26
Nesbanebdjed 36

Osorkon II *22,36*

Pepy I 19,27
Pepy II 19,27
Peribsen 23,24
Philip Arrhidaeus 40
Piankhi 37
Psamtek I *18,40*
Psamtek II 39
Ptolemy I (son of Lagus) 40,41
Ptolemy III 40
Ptolemy IV 40
Ptolemy V 40
Ptolemy VII *41*
Ptolemy XII 40,41

Qa'a 22

Ramses I 34
Ramses II *11*,33,34,*34*,35,36,39
Ramses III 9,35
Ramses IV *12*
Ramses XI 35,36
Ro 21

Sahura 17
Scorpion 21
Sekhemib 24
Semerkhet 22,23
Senusret I 10,*28*,29,39
Senusret II 29
Senusret III 15,30,*30*
Seqenenra Taa 31
Sety I 34,35,*35*
Shabako 37
Shabitko 37
Shepseskaf *26*
Sneferu 25,*25*

Taharqo *36*,37
Tanutamani 37
Thutmose I 11,12,13,*13*,14,31
Thutmose II 14
Thutmose III 13,14,*14*,15,16
Tiberius *42*
Titus 43
Tutankhamun 32

Userkaf 17